THE NEXT TANGO

A PATIENT GUIDE

THE NEXT TANGO

All you need to know to deliver
great results in health care

HANNA BOËTHIUS

VERENA VOELTER, MD

(EDITORS)

GRAMMAR
FACTORY
— ESTᴰ 2013 —

TESTIMONIALS

This book is essential reading for both patients and healthcare professionals. With their unique ability to weave personal patient stories alongside evidence-based, data-driven research, Dr Verena Voelter and Hanna Boëthius reimagine our healthcare system with clarity and insight. As an ER doctor myself, I'm often reminded that one day, I will navigate this system as a patient—a dreadful thought given the dysfunction I see today. This book is a vital guide for all of us. It shows how we can work together toward the real solutions that *The Next Tango* authors propose. Amid the challenges we face, their hopeful vision is precisely what we need right now.

Andrea Austin, MD
Author of *Revitalized: A Guidebook to Following Your Healing Heartline*
Podcast host of *Heartline: Changemaking in Healthcare*

Verena and Hanna's focus on patient-centered partnerships that involve all actors across health care is spot on. Only a well-coordinated dance between pharma, payers, policymakers, healthcare professionals, and patients can catalyze the much-needed shift from reactive care systems to proactive, predictive, and preventive health systems that keep people healthy. The symphony of today's vast amounts of health data, combined with advanced analytical capabilities, has the potential to provide the rhythm for this dance.

Ann Aerts, MD
Head of the Novartis Foundation

The Next Tango is an inspirational book. It brings real-world examples that showcase the necessity of all the stakeholders to dance a tango that brings patients to the centerstage of care. The book recognizes how legacy business models involving payers, pharma, and providers—if not aligned by value agreements—do actually *not* achieve patient-centered value. However, that *should* precisely be the purpose of those organizations. The book serves as a guide to do it differently. For people who work with healthcare strategy and policy, it makes us travel across healthcare systems' problems and identify opportunities for building better solutions that can impact population health and keep organizations sustainable.

Prof. Dr Ana Paula Beck da Silva Etges
Adjunct Professor at the Federal University of Rio Grande do Sul
Co-founder of the TDABC in Healthcare Consortium
Board member of PEV Healthcare Consulting

With *The Next Tango*, Ms Boëthius, Dr Voelter, and co-authors foster greater understanding among all stakeholders of patient interests in health care—not as the other stakeholders want to understand them, but as the *patients themselves* wish subjectively to be understood. This empathetic appreciation, expressed through each of the other stakeholders' perspectives, is essential to unlock the full potential of a healthcare system that today rapidly evolves with burgeoning change in science, public policy, and finance. A stakeholder who can readily and sincerely inhabit the patient's point of view can not only generate more value for the patient, but enlist the patient's cooperation for the benefit of the whole system. We all thereby raise the standard of care—for one another.

Charles Barker LLM
Managing director of PrimeMover Associates
Collaboration and Conflict Management

Patient centricity is a logical next step for 5P healthcare leaders' collaborative value creation. The focus on patient outcomes is very important for *all-in* health care delivery today, replacing legacy systems and leaders stuck in self-interest and seeking to hang on to the status quo. *The Next Tango* is a highly recommended read for those who want to do the right thing for patients and their loved ones.

Prof. Dr Fred van Eenennaam
President and chairman of VBHC Center Europe
and The Decision Institute

The Next Tango brilliantly captures the shifting landscape of patient-centered health care. It shows how regulatory bodies and policymakers have become strategic partners in an essential, yet complex interplay between rigorous data evaluation and the need to address diverse patient needs. This balancing act can create tension with other stakeholders, such as providers and payers, whose priorities are broad access and cost efficiency. The authors elegantly embrace this dynamic tension—rather than defaulting to criticism—and propose a song sheet to foster collaboration and achieving the best possible outcomes for patients.

Katrin Rupalla, PhD, MBA
Head of global regulatory affairs at Johnson &
Johnson Innovative Medicine and
Former board member of the Cancer Drug Development Forum

What a great book. I really enjoyed how the authors put the emphasis on the patient perspective! Particularly the *partisan perceptions* with empathy toward all five actors—this is central to the understanding of why we all act in different ways in health care. The last chapter provides a blueprint of doing this in real life: putting it together in *The Next Tango*.

Lars Nicklasson
Market access and healthcare
public affairs professional

I love this book! It's a clear agenda for change that will lead to a meaningful and productive dance for the people who seek care as well as those who provide care. All throughout, I see the need for my favorite song about healthcare today—we all need Sia's "*Courage to Change*." It doesn't have to be scary. Change can be creative. It can be liberating. But the one thing change cannot be is incremental. Small, random steps will not create the tango Verena Voelter and Hanna Boëthius imagine. *The Next Tango* they envision is integrated with members of the dance troupe moving in sync. As Sia's song continues, "*You're not alone, I promise. Standing together we can do anything.*"

Stephen K. Klasko, MD, MBA
Former CEO of Jefferson Health
Author of *Patient No Longer* and *Feelin' Alright*

The Next Tango is a rare book that is co-authored by diverse stakeholders in health care—including a patient. It asks the crucial question, "*How do we get the 'care' back into health care?*" This timely book contains evidence that while health care is teetering on a global collapse, the system offers little value for suffering patients and beleaguered staff. The authors impart an understanding of the roles of the various actors in health care. *The Next Tango* refreshingly centers on the often-forgotten patient and is a must-read for anybody who advocates for health system improvement.

Sue Robins
Patient advocate and speaker, Author of *Bird's Eye View: Stories of*
a life lived in health care* and *Ducks in a Row: Health Care Reimagined

Published by Grammar Factory Publishing, an imprint of MacMillan Company Limited.

Grammar Factory Publishing
MacMillan Company Limited
25 Telegram Mews, 39th Floor, Suite 3906
Toronto, Ontario, Canada
M5V 3Z1

www.grammarfactory.com

Boëthius, Hanna and Verena Voelter, MD.
The Next Tango: A Patient Guide: All You Need to Know to Deliver Great Results in Health Care / Hanna Boëthius and Verena Voelter, MD.

Paperback ISBN 978-1-998528-17-2
eBook ISBN 978-1-998528-18-9

1. BUS010170 BUSINESS & ECONOMICS / Industries / Healthcare.
2. MED037000 MEDICAL / Health Risk Assessment.
3. MED035000 MEDICAL / Health Care Delivery.

Production Credits
Cover design by Designerbility
Interior layout design by Setareh Ashrafologhalai
Book production and editorial services by Grammar Factory Publishing

Grammar Factory's Carbon Neutral Publishing Commitment

Disclaimer

I dedicate this book to the incredibly inspiring Diabetes Online Community, which has helped me through both good and bad times living with this condition 24/7/365. Also to the amazingly compassionate providers that I have met throughout my "diabetic career."

To my beloved husband, Sebastian, who stands steadily beside me through thick and thin. My family and friends, who cheer me on in all types of weather.

Thank you for dancing the tango of life with me.

HANNA BOËTHIUS

My deepest gratitude goes to my cancer patients.

They have taught me humility and a view on what's essential:

being human and feeling connected. This book is for them.

I feel blessed that I can continue to give back from my various facets of health care experience. With gratitude to my amazing colleagues at 5P Health Care Solutions, and to my tango partner in life, Roger, who balances my mental sanity 24/7/365—I love you.

VERENA VOELTER

Contents

ABOUT THE EDITORS

HANNA BOËTHIUS, MSc

Having lived almost her entire life with type 1 diabetes, Hanna has grown up with "the patient" as part of her persona. This has helped guide her life's mission—to help others live a better and healthier life (with or without a chronic condition in tow), which she has realized through various certifications, projects, and positions as an expert patient voice. In her role as a consultant at 5P Health Care Solutions, she focuses on patient empowerment.

The insight that no stakeholder can be 'the one' to catalyze change in health care was further crystallized when meeting Verena and acting as a sounding board for her first book, *TangoForFive*. Since then, their collaboration has evolved into changing health care together as the ultimate patient-provider duo, helping to choreograph the intricate tango of health care actors. Hanna is profoundly thankful to Verena for enabling her to live her "why," to her family and friends ("type F") who are always supportive of her efforts, as well as to the ever changing world of health care, indicating that change, indeed, is possible.

VERENA VOELTER, MD

As a trained internist and oncologist, Dr Voelter has always seen her role at the side of the patient. Since the publication of her first book, *TangoForFive*, she has participated in numerous conversations with interested readers and members of the 5P ecosystem on how to make this vision of cooperation a reality. Patients, fellow doctors, policymakers, and health insurers, as well as leaders from the pharmaceutical industry and life sciences, have supported her in breaking down silos and championing a *TangoForFive* as the holy grail to fix our ailing health systems.

Verena's encounter with Hanna has been a gamechanger on that journey. This book wouldn't exist without the endless hours they spent together, focusing on how they can help their fellow tango dancers on the health care stage perform better. Verena's deepest gratitude goes to Hanna, to the countless like-minded change agents across the tango of health care who share their vision, and to her family. As the founder of 5P Health Care Solutions, Dr Voelter provides consulting and coaching services to all players in the healthcare ecosystem, and provides motivational keynote lectures and panel moderations, always wearing the hat of the neutral broker to catalyze public-private partnerships in health care with the goal of achieving joint value creation.

Why patient centricity matters

By Hanna Boëthius and Verena Voelter

*"Health care is the most difficult,
chaotic, and complex industry to manage."*

~ PETER DRUCKER

In 2020, I (Verena) wrote *TangoForFive*—a book about the ailings and failings of our current healthcare systems, and ideas on how to make health care a better place through cooperation rather than competition.[1] Having spent three decades providing and developing care myself, I was frustrated with the finger pointing going on around perceived high drug prices, greedy payers, and doctors-turned-robots becoming overly reliant on screens and keyboards. Meanwhile, the ultimate customer in health care—the patient—seemed to fall off the radar altogether.

In 2024, and one pandemic later, we issue *The Next Tango*, integrating the learnings and new trends on the horizon of healthcare system transformation. Together with Hanna Boëthius, a lifelong patient expert and empowerment consultant, we aim to give a voice to the patient by focusing on what matters most: the best outcomes for patients at the lowest cost for the system.

This book, just like *TangoForFive*, includes perspectives from all other actors that make up the fabric of health care: the tango of the 5P value chain. To recap, the 5Ps are:

- **Patients** receiving care
- **Providers** providing care
- **Pharma**, MedTech and life sciences developing care
- **Payers** paying for care
- **Policymakers** providing the regulatory and ethical framework for that care

Patients and doctors interacting and co-creating care plans is the center of gravity in health care, as we see it. No doctor-patient relationship, no health care. Yet, in a legacy system that rewards and pays for procedures, pills, and processes, what you get is more of the same: more procedures, more pills, and more processes. It is generally referred to as fee-for-service (FFS). The problem with it?

The patient isn't part of that vocabulary, nor are best outcomes for patients part of those incentives!

The consequences are clearly spelled out in today's headlines: hospitals and health systems failing and going bankrupt, and countries claiming that medicine overall is too expensive.[2] All while health care workers turn away from their original jobs and passion, due to burnout—exacerbated by the pandemic—and the pressure to produce in *relative value unit* (RVU) systems. Rather than living in a system that favors the time spent with patients, providers are expected to see even more patients, and complete more procedures per time unit, in order to make the money equation work. It's no surprise, then, that neither patients nor providers feel valued.[1]

On a global scale, health care is one of the most—if not *the* most—inefficient industry overall. To depict this, the much referred to OECD (Organisation for Economic Co-operation and Development) two-way graph in figure i shows a recent update of healthcare spending per capita versus life expectancy in a purchasing power normalized plot per country.

Figure i: The broken balance between innovation and affordability: life expectancy versus healthcare spending (per capita and purchase power corrected) in selected OECD countries; available at www. oecd.com—data last accessed August 2024. Arrows depict changes since 2019 for three countries: the USA, Switzerland, (CHE), and France (FRA). Note: Since 2021, UK data has been unavailable in the OECD database, so an alternative data source was used.

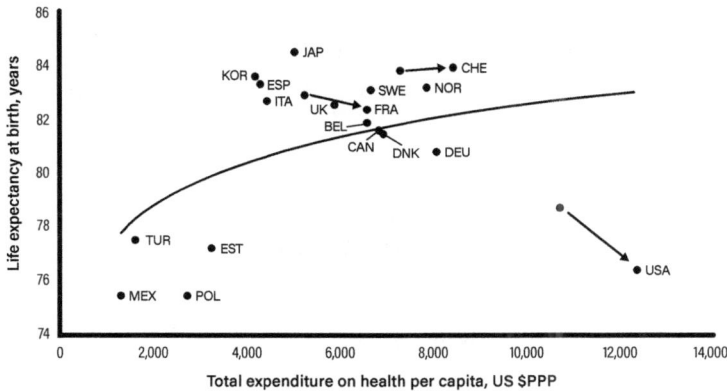

While there is a wide range from Poland (slightly less than seventy-six years of life expectancy for about 3,000 dollars spent per person) to the US (slightly more than seventy-six years of life expectancy but more than 12,000 dollars per person), the dimension you do not see in this graph is the third one: the one of time. The overall growth of healthcare spending per GDP (gross domestic product) year over year is reaching an average of 9.2 per cent compared to 8.8 per cent five years ago, now with a range of 2.9 per cent (India) to 16.6 per cent (US).[1, 2] It keeps deepening the schisms of health care with continued cost pressures on all actors of the value chain, leading to provider and hospital inefficiencies, health plans with skewed budgets, pharma pressure on topline and drug discovery pipelines, tightened patient out-of-pocket premiums, and country policymakers scratching their heads on how to deliver innovative and effective care while keeping it all affordable. In sharp contrast, life expectancy has been stalling for over a decade, and has even taken a reverse trend in recent years. Even before COVID-19, the world's top economy, the US, had been experiencing shortened lifespans each year since 2015.[5]

In no other industry would such a negative margin on a balance sheet of topline free-falling outcomes versus bottom-line skyrocketing cost be acceptable.

If you are a general manager and showing this margin, you are likely to get fired.

What we have noticed since *TangoForFive*, and one pandemic later, is that while there are positive trends on the horizon, with lots of new initiatives and pilot projects, some gaps and traps still continue to grow larger. On the one hand, what is commonly referred to as Value-Based Health Care (VBHC)—in other words, putting incentives upside-down and rewarding outcomes that matter to patients instead of paying for pills and procedures—is clearly on the upward trend, powered by the potential of the digital revolution. We have had the honor of interviewing twelve visionary organizations embarking on this transformation, from FFS to VBHC, worldwide.[6] In short, among the top five focus areas for action—organization, people, resources, data, implementation—clearly, the overarching theme identified was the importance of executive leadership. Mingling with teams, understanding both patients' and doctors' concerns on a daily basis, and empowering grassroot initiatives has shown to bring true progress. Coupled with holding everyone accountable, including incentives on quality for all employees (starting with the C-suite!), this is what will help executives of hospitals, pharma companies, insurers, and health authorities become more successful. We believe that a focus on patient outcomes will inject more care into healthcare.

When it comes to the feasibility of making an executive VBHC transformation happen, one of our role models is Dr Stephen K Klasko, who has demonstrated exactly that as the former CEO at Jefferson Health. Recently, Dr Klasko summarized that industry leaders must start thinking about changes that will truly transform health care, a vision of *"health care at any address."*[7, 8] Demonstrating the need for cross-sector collaboration, he equally dedicates his effort to get payers, providers, and tech companies to partner further to help patients more. In his latest book, *Feelin' Alright: How the Message in the Music Can Make Healthcare Healthier*, which is a must-read for all healthcare change agents, the theme of music deeply resonates with our tango steps approach to healthcare transformation.[9]

On the other hand, more often than not, patients are still not consistently at the center of the proverbial round table and care team—with hospitals being built and billed around siloed departments that suit the administrative flow better than a patient's journey.

A patient who is trying to navigate what looks like a stressful hurdles race is still more common today than a pleasant customer experience in, for example, a fancy restaurant or a Nike flagship store that revolves all around the consumer's needs, well-being, and enjoyment.

As outlined in *TangoForFive*, the healthcare business model is hyper complex and siloed.[1] During lectures, Verena generally refers to it as a "B2B2B2B2C model"—aligned with the 5P concept. Picture this: although you as the patient are the ultimate customer and beneficiary of the service, you never chose to be sick in the first place. Secondly, you typically don't pick the medicine yourself because you have no idea nor wish for it. Thirdly, you don't directly buy the medicine because someone else does that for you—a provider and a payer. Odd, isn't it? Yet, actors in health care behave in silos and try to reap maximum benefits without looking right nor left in the value chain, nor to the patient's best outcome.

The main barrier to effectively breaking down silos in health care is what we generally refer to as *partisan perceptions* (figure ii). Without going into too much detail at this early stage in the book (it is the topic of the concluding chapter), it is enough to say here that failure to understand each other's real-life situations and constraints across the 5P value chain is the *number one* reason for lack of progress in health care.

Figure ii: The trap of partisan perceptions. Failing to see behind "the curtain", discovering what is really going on in someone else's life, often holds us hostage. Pulling back that curtain with curiosity opens up new perspectives on the other health care leaders, including their interests, problems, and constraints, and hence fosters collaboration and joint value creation instead of silos and value destruction.

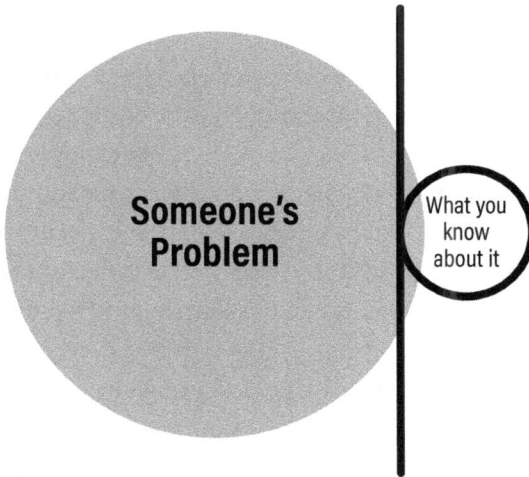

The purpose of this book is to remedy this by giving a voice to each of the five main actors along the value chain and, as a result, starting to understand what their interests and needs are. What is clear is that no one is lacking the motivation and willingness to collaborate! What we are missing is a clear song sheet that allows us to see what is possible together. This involves pulling back that curtain with regard to what other specialty actors in health care (pharma, payer, and policy, for example) want and need, but also going deeper on what is the backbone of health care: the patient-provider relationship and how more participation from both sides can lead to better outcomes for patients.

Today, health care is like a business—
yet they forget about the patient.

Before we go any further, a quick question: What's the difference between *"healthcare"* and *"health care"*?

The former is typically used to describe a healthcare *system* that is governed within a country or a region. The latter is putting the emphasis on the word *"care"*, and therefore alludes to more of an individual context—the patient receiving care and the provider providing care. (Oddly enough, the notion of *quality* of care in a health*care* system rewarding *quantities* of care is not the primary incentive, as stated earlier in the context of FFS pitfalls.)

So, the crystal ball question is: How can we inject more *care* into *healthcare*? How can we make it a more individualized, patient-centric system that also brings rewards to all 5P actors equally? In other words, how can we bring that kind of pleasant restaurant or Nike flagship store experience to patients who are in need of health *care*, and for providers delivering that best *quality* care? We believe that a collaborative, outcomes-based system—which incentivizes and rewards the best possible results for patients—is the future for resilient and cost-effective systems. Making that a practical reality is the key topic of *The Next Tango*.

WHAT YOU CAN EXPECT FROM THIS BOOK

The Next Tango is an educational tool. It provides the interested reader with a toolbox of explanations and background information to understand more about the other sectors along the value chain.

It helps to pull back that curtain just a bit more and see beyond our own reality and scope of expertise as we realize that no one actor alone can know everything required to fix those complex issues in health care. This book delivers ample resources and opportunities to pause and reflect. By adding a reflection box with a set of questions at the end of each chapter, it assists readers, including those working in any health care sector, to reflect on what each and every one of us can do differently. Very practically. And very immediately.

Figure iii: Structure of The Next Tango. Following the logic of the health care value chain, the book offers perspectives of Patients in Chapter 1; participative research by Providers in Chapter 2; joint value creation through public-private partnerships by Pharma in Chapter 3; sharing risks and co-creating value contracts with Payers in Chapter 4; and how Policymakers develop frameworks to support patient-centric, coordinated, and smart care in Chapter 5. All of this is anchored in the last chapter, titled "The Fabric of Dancing a Collaborative Tango in Health Care", which outlines seven steps to effective multi-party collaboration (MPC).

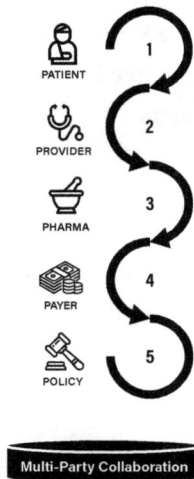

We feel fortunate to be part of this growing author community of real-life health care leaders dancing the tango of collaboration along the 5P value chain. The authors featured in the coming chapters all come with their own individual styles and themes. No one pretends to speak on behalf of all their constituents. We invite you, the reader, to reflect on their perspectives to stimulate your own curiosity and creativity for novel solutions in each area of responsibility.

What makes The Next Tango unique is the wonderful set of voices provided by true experts in their fields.

Who are the authors of *The Next Tango*?

As a trained internist-oncologist and author of *TangoForFive*, Dr Verena Voelter brings her unique views as a provider, while drawing on her pharma executive past and her expertise as a negotiator coach. As stated earlier, she is also the founder and CEO of 5P Health Care Solutions, a boutique health care consulting firm that catalyzes public-private partnerships.

Hanna Boëthius was featured as a core contributor in *Tango-ForFive* and acts as a patient expert with a scientific and clinical background in diabetes care management. As stated earlier, she also serves as a consultant at 5P Health Care Solutions, with a focus on patient empowerment.

As the co-editors and primary authors of *The Next Tango*, Verena and Hanna role model that ideal tango-like doctor-patient relationship by bringing an eye-to-eye, respectful spin to the concept of care coordination for outcomes that matter—to patients and to all 5P actors in the system. In Chapter 1, Hanna shares her specialized knowledge and perspective in more detail.

In Chapter 2, Dr Claudia Witt and Claudia Canella bring a unique set of experiences from a promising new field referred to as *participative research*. It brings to life novel tools and perspectives enabling real-life co-creation between actively empowered patients and their families.

In Chapter 3, long-time pharmaceutical leader Nienke Feenstra is the best choice to contribute with her compelling views on how drug development and commercialization play a unique role in powering public-private partnerships toward value creation and better outcomes.

In Chapter 4, accompanied by Verena, Caitlin Masters wraps up the patient-centric journey with deep insights into ways to partner on paying for health care—a much-needed perspective to redirect dead-end pricing conversations toward what matters most: sustainable outcomes for patients and better value for all.

In Chapter 5, which features the critical view of Dr Paul Sherrington, the reader learns about the role of policy in the 21st century, and the numerous initiatives that call for engagement and co-creation by various health authorities around the world.

Lastly, facts and legitimacy are good to understand. But they fall short if we can't bridge our opposing interests. The final chapter shares the expertise of Dr Suzanne Robinson, a fellow alumna to Verena from the Harvard Negotiation Project, who puts it all into context via the seven steps of dancing a tango of multi-party collaboration (MPC).

The Next Tango is a practical book. It provides you with ample concrete ideas on what you can do differently in your day job, no matter where you are in the 5P ecosystem. We know that only together we become stronger—as no one actor alone can fix the problems that plague health care today.

Ready? Let's continue to dance!

Verena Voelter and Hanna Boëthius
Zürich, November 2024

A song sheet for individual satisfaction and value generation in health care

By Hanna Boëthius and Verena Voelter

"Happy employees ensure happy customers. And happy customers ensure happy stakeholders—in that order."

~ SIMON SINEK

If we use this brilliant quote by Simon Sinek and change the words "employees" to "providers," "customers" to "patients," and "stakeholders" to "payer/pharma/policy," we start to see a pattern. We believe patients are immensely powerful and ultimately determine how health care is delivered.

Let's kick it off with a real-life story from Verena to underpin what we are up to here.

On a Friday in December, despite watching snowflakes falling outside the window, I am plagued by hot flashes. It is a week before my birthday. Why am I hot when it is so cold outside? Confused, I am sitting in a day-clinic chair, receiving a novel therapy for my chronic autoimmune condition. The therapy lasts four hours, and I am incapacitated by an IV lane on my hand. I'm reflecting. My doctors told me this would be the most modern, most effective therapy available for my condition, and praised it like a gold bar presented for my birthday.

Yet, no one informed me of the logistics around it: that I'm tied to a chair; that I should have brought audiobooks rather than my computer to work on or books to read; that the pre-medication has potentially more side effects than the innovative remedy itself. (Not to mention the inconvenience in the weeks prior of having two different providers each take their own blood draws because they wouldn't trust each other's reference labs. What was the cost again for that duplication? To complicate things further, those lab results were not available on a centralized electronic health record in Switzerland!) As it turned out, it was the hundreds of milligrams of cortisone flooding my body that resulted in what felt like an LSD trip (I swear, I never had one!). Half a day later, I was released onto the streets. Thankfully I had chosen to take the train in the morning and not my car. I would have crashed it with all that dope! (No one advised me on that—it had been just my own gut feeling.)

I was texting Hanna from the train: "*It's over.*"

Suddenly, the pressure and hot flashes released like feathers into the wind as I was pulling my hat and scarf tighter amid the falling snow. "*I feel like I can manage again—there's this power kicking in,*" I wrote to her. "*Now, I think I'll go to Bahnhofstrasse and get myself that overpriced fancy new handbag I've been eyeballing lately—I'll just do it! Screw the money.*" And then Hanna said what would turn into the key trigger for this *Next Tango*: "*Verena, I love that! Go for it! It's all about self-care—that is so important. I'm a huge fan. Go and get that bag and give yourself a treat! You deserve it.*"

Bam. There's that word—"care"—again. And "self-care"? What a
revolutionary concept. I replied: *"Hanna: we've got our next book!"*

Allow me (Hanna) to provide some context here.

As I was answering Verena, I was reflecting on my own lifelong
journey as an insulin-dependent patient. When you are "the
patient," especially of the chronic variety, the reality is that only
you can figure out what fits you, your body, and your situation
the best. You have to sustain the energy to keep on top of your
treatments, including the ever-evolving options that may be available, and when you should interact with what provider (or policy,
pharma or payer, for that matter). "You are always your own best
doctor," my mother would tell me since the age of two when I was
diagnosed with type 1 diabetes (T1D), an autoimmune condition
that means the beta cells in my pancreas can't produce any insulin,
which happens to be the body's master hormone. How do you
navigate a lifetime of energy-robbing illness, perhaps not even due
to the condition itself, but rather the exhausting task of navigating
a broken healthcare system, where "care" seems to be optional?

To simplify, you need to find glimmers of self-care, as outlined
at the end of Verena's story. While it doesn't have to be a bucket
list item, such as a handbag, it's important to be kind to yourself
when steering through life as a patient. Whether it's as simple as
taking yourself out for a coffee, spoiling yourself with a beauty
treatment, watching your favorite show or movie, seeing a concert,
going for a walk in the forest or on the beach, or, indeed, investing
in a bucket list item, it's about acknowledging that you have faced
another milestone on your health care journey in the form of a
treatment, visit, blood draw, scan... No one is going to pat you on

the back (although amazing lived experience communities, as well as supportive friends and family, can help a lot!).

As a patient, you've only got yourself, and that hero needs to be treated as such.

We'll dive deeper into what you can do as a patient to care for yourself, increase your health literacy (and hence empower yourself more), and boost your listening skills in the upcoming chapters. Here, I want to touch on the idea of the "round table," as it pertains to the most important relationship of patient centricity: the one with your health care provider, aka your doctor and your nurse.

This idea was first introduced in *TangoForFive*, namely in Chapter 3. The proverbial round table, or your medical dream team, is where you, as the patient, have the seat of honor alongside your health care providers in order to co-create and achieve health goals together. This team of experts differs depending on the condition you live with, and you'll get a sense of that complexity in Chapter 1. It's a big team that needs coordination, communication, and collaboration. And guess who normally gets the honor of doing that? Yes, that would be you, the patient (as if living with a condition isn't difficult enough!).

The beauty of care coordination around patient needs and outcomes is that it catalyzes teamwork.

Once you focus on the customer's needs and start working toward solving a problem for them, while creating the best possible experience, you start creating value. In the context of health care, this is individual power turned into system power. Ample examples show us that what is right for the patient is right for the system because it carves out waste such as unnecessary diagnostics, therapies, and repeat exams.[1]

Let's talk about the notion of waste for a minute as it is a cornerstone in the need for change.

Why is this still *the* big elephant in the room, as highlighted in *TangoForFive*? The issue at hand: thirty to fifty per cent of any healthcare dollar or euro spent is wasted, as we will discuss in much more detail in Chapter 4. But just to make it a visual and concrete example here: for a healthcare budget of about 300 billion euros, like in France, that would mean 100 to 150 billion euros are wasted—thrown out the window. How much innovation and patient-centric care could be financed with even 100 million of whatever currency we are asking for?

Tapping into the biggest lever of healthcare expenditure, getting a grasp on waste should be our collective top priority.

The main sources of wasteful spending have been analyzed by many. The most widely cited 2017 OECD report, "Tackling Wasteful Spending on Health", has categorized inefficient healthcare spending into three main categories (figure iv): *clinical* (over- and under-care); *operational* (duplication of testing and inefficient resource utilization); and *fraud* (administration, corruption, and infrastructure).[10] While we have not been able to identify an update to this landmark analysis—particularly in the aftermath of the pandemic—a US study from 2019 provides additional legitimacy on why handling waste represents an opportunity to bend the curve on spending. This meta-analysis of fifty-four studies projected potential savings from eliminating waste, ranging from 191 billion dollars to 286 billion dollars, representing a potential twenty-five per cent reduction in the total cost of waste.[11]

Figure iv: Three main categories of healthcare waste worldwide.

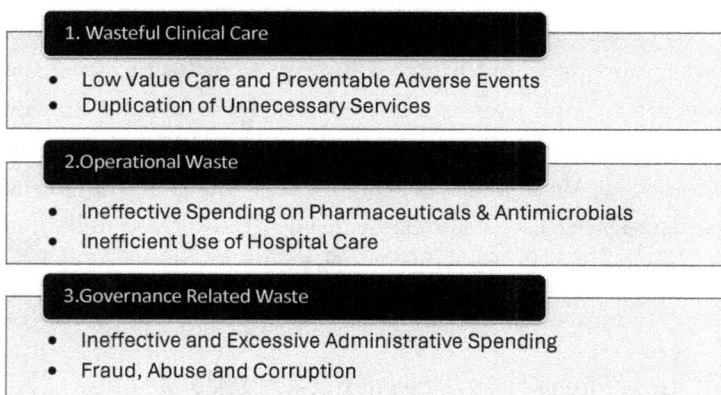

1. Wasteful Clinical Care
- Low Value Care and Preventable Adverse Events
- Duplication of Unnecessary Services

2. Operational Waste
- Ineffective Spending on Pharmaceuticals & Antimicrobials
- Inefficient Use of Hospital Care

3. Governance Related Waste
- Ineffective and Excessive Administrative Spending
- Fraud, Abuse and Corruption

Source[10]

Back in 2006, Michael Porter and Elizabeth Teisberg introduced a remedy to these inefficient ways of working: Value-Based Health Care (VBHC).

In their seminal book *Redefining Health Care*, they outlined a seemingly simple, yet complex definition: Value = Outcomes / Cost.[12] Simple, because, in only three words, it translates into health care language what Simon Sinek teaches us from a customer-centric marketing standpoint: focus on the results that matter to your customers, and cost efficiencies will follow. Complex, because there is no one-size-fits-all way to measure an entire cycle of care and related cost across the current 5P patient journey.

This is where we come full circle with the proverbial round table to what we both describe in our own patient-centric life experiences.

VBHC holds the power to break down silos along the patient journey. It pulls together all actors needed to deliver best possible results that matter to patients, and it brings everyone onto the same page.

With VBHC, there is no more left hand not knowing what the right hand does. No more useless duplication of tests and exams because the patient's GP (general practitioner) does not communicate with the patient's endocrinologist. No more costly pills and procedures if the patient only needs a massage to alleviate their pain (a real lived experience by Verena!). There are many more examples to tell here—and you as a reader may have your own to share. What we do see is that a focus on probing, listening, and co-creating solutions that cater to what the patient actually wants leads to substantial team satisfaction, better patient experience, and system efficiencies overall. For the interested reader, we refer you to the great resource center that is Value-Based Healthcare Center Europe, which, every year, awards the most promising new VBHC initiative internationally.[13]

In short, we conclude that *"we don't have a problem of resource shortages in health care—but an issue of resources in the wrong place."*[1] Although this is still a reality broadly speaking, the good news is that we see small, but impactful steps in the right direction to correct the pattern of waste from over- and under-care to a more meaningful approach to spending for outcomes that really matter.

As a carrot for care coordination and collaboration toward outcomes that matter to patients, VBHC comes with a proven benefit for providers as well!

By spending more time with the patient, and by being able to coordinate solutions that really matter to the patient, doctors and nurses are brought closer to their original vocation: to provide care. Legacy FFS with nuisance RVU frameworks and their pressure to produce have stripped providers of their most valuable commodity: time. Time for patients. Time to reflect. Time to care for themselves. The US Surgeon General Dr Vivek Murthy has made it a national priority by issuing a white paper and respective taskforce, titled "Addressing Health Worker Burnout."[14, 15] Praised in the early days of the pandemic as healthcare heroes, the focus on keeping health care workers healthy weaned off quickly as normalcy and pressure to produce kicked back in. Hence, Dr Murthy's advisory is an impressive and comprehensive 5P overview on what everyone in the ecosystem can contribute to safeguard health care workers so they can do their jobs well.

A transformed system built on the principles of VBHC coordinates new ways of working around the true needs of the patient by carving out wasted resources—money, people, time. That time is given back to where it's needed the most: at the heart of health care, the patient-doctor relationship.

Research has shown that linking your work to your inner self leads to more fulfilling work experiences and happier lives altogether.[17] *"Stop surviving and start flourishing,"* writes Sharee Johnson in her bestseller book *The Thriving Doctor*.[13] This requires time. As a trained psychologist and leader in physician-coaching, Sharee deeply understands the flaws introduced by the system, and the impact of FFS on physician burnout and health care worker shortages. In her work, she co-creates strategies that enable an effective framework of *self-care* for doctors once that quality time kicks back in. It entails building the right habits to strengthen the skillset of self-regulation, such as clarity of mind, emotional literacy, and self-awareness. Her book comes as a highly recommended practical guide helping doctors to get ahead of stress curves referred to as "HALLTSS" (figure v). Every doctor on a busy ward has experienced at least one of those feelings, if not all of them: hungry, angry, lonely, late, tired, stressed, and becoming sick.

Figure v: HALLTSS—self-care for doctors.

© Sharee Johnson, *The Thriving Doctor*, Source[16]

As a doctor myself (Verena), the notion of cultivating emotional literacy has particularly struck me as I'm reading Sharee's book one more time. *"The idea that doctors can suppress their emotions"* is a real concern as the academic machinery produces a highly competitive workforce that focuses on tech more than humans in delivering laser-focused diagnoses and finding the most innovative medicine.[18] It is refreshing to see the trend of more and more doctors speaking up, caring for themselves, and sharing experiences in the community, such as the latest book by Dr Andrea Austin, titled *Revitalized: A Guidebook to Following Your Healing Heartline.*[19]

However, doctor trainings today don't place enough emphasis on emotions nor aspects of humanistic care, as only a minority of training curriculum is devoted to what is generally referred to as *soft skills*. In light of the digital revolution with chatbots, ChatGPT, and other fancy gadgets that are filling our pockets and wrists, there is a real risk of inter-human basic soft skills becoming more of an afterthought than a front-and-center requirement. "The Future of Jobs Report 2023", issued by the World Economic Forum and based on a survey of 803 companies covering more than eleven million employees across twenty-seven industries, emphasizes the increasingly competitive role of cognitive functions such as creative thinking, resilience, flexibility, agility, motivation, self-awareness, curiosity, and lifelong learning.[20]

It is time to bring these critical human skills back home to the most human of all industries: health care.

Yes, much of health care is chaotic, submitted to megatrends (keyword: pandemic) and wildly interconnected trends from other happenings across borders (keyword: wars). These are vastly outside of our control. What we do have in our control, though, is the focus on ourselves and the direct intersections we navigate on a daily basis. Self-care for patients, self-care for doctors, and care coordination for best outcomes are the foundational steps for a successful tango in health care.

As we've stated several times now, we're all for bringing more *care* into healthcare. And all of it is in our direct reach.

What you will discover in the following chapters is the role that each of the five most crucial actors on the health care scene can play to collectively bring the theme of patient centricity to life. For patients' benefit, front and center. And for the system's benefit as well.

Curious about what you can do to enable this?

Let's move on.

CHAPTER 1

The *Patient* view on outcomes that matter and how we get there

By Hanna Boëthius

"One day you will tell your story of how you overcame what you went through, and it will be someone else's survival guide."

~ BRENÉ BROWN

Growing up by the ocean was one of those incredible privileges you only really appreciate once you no longer live there. The smell of salty water, the sound of the waves, and the occasional ray of sunshine on your face. Bliss—and truly my happy place still today! Talk about self-care.

I'm also privileged to still be alive with a chronic condition and witness the technological revolution that has happened in the past forty years. From boiling my syringe needles to sterilize them and having to sharpen them myself (!) when they got dull, I now have access to insulin pumps and continuous glucose measuring technology that can be steered through an app. That is wild, and a very impactful privilege!

With scientific literature, including journals such as the *British Medical Journal* and *Diabetologia*, dedicating entire issues to patient-led content, as well as patient-centric questions derived from patient communities, there is no better time to highlight the importance of patient centricity in a system-wide context.[21, 22]

While my personal journey of self-care as a patient is essential, it becomes even more meaningful when the entire healthcare system supports and facilitates my efforts. This chapter reflects on how other health care stakeholders—providers, payers, pharma, policymakers, together with society—can support the patient journey, making it easier and more effective.

Figure 1.1: The importance of collaboration in the patient-provider relationship.

"Relax — we're all in this together."

It's time to give a voice to the patients, so let's talk more about the powerful role patients have in the healthcare system, what we can do to amplify that role, and, yes, more beach analogies!

Ready?

THE JOURNEY OF SELF-ADVOCACY

Living as a young child with type 1 diabetes (T1D) in the 1980s was a very different story than it would be today. We had primitive care tools in the form of syringes and stiff, flat dosing of insulin, twice per day at exactly the same/right time. Some might say it was a management regimen unfit for a kid, especially if you think of any spontaneity, swimming, biking, dancing... How do you possibly try to master turbulent blood sugar levels with the same regimen that you would use to treat an eighty-year-old with type 2 diabetes (T2D)? An insulin pump? A glucose meter? An app to help me monitor both glucose and insulin? Dream on... The solutions available to us today weren't even part of our imagination back then.

Additionally, the very old-fashioned culture in medicine ruled, where doctors were like gods in white coats, and patients and their families were spoken to from top down—literally. Picture this: my parents showing up with their five-year-old, proudly holding their carefully handwritten diary, showcasing glucose levels each hour of the day for the past three months (shockingly, this is common practice even today!). Only for the doctor to snap, *"A blood sugar of 17 mmol/l on April 1st at 5pm, seriously? That should not have happened. What did you do wrong?"* This attitude left my parents, and the whole family, feeling ashamed and helpless. They deserved better! None of this was their wrongdoing. Rather, it was thanks to a lack of insight and proper understanding of the condition by all actors.

As a patient navigating the complex world of health care across several countries, I have now learned that taking charge of my health is not just a choice—it's a necessity. I've been mansplained to about my own care by many, felt misunderstood, sidelined, and spoken about rather than to. Decisions have been made without my input or consent, reimbursements have been denied, treatment options not mentioned, and judgments made about my behaviors. Because they "knew better". I think you can sense the pattern—the patient has historically not been part of the vocabulary in classical FFS systems. Perhaps you have experienced similar situations yourself? And as Sue Robins states in her book, *Ducks in a Row: Health Care Reimagined*, *"Health care is about caring for humans—there is a messiness that goes along with that."*[23] I think this beautifully summarizes what's needed; the human touch in health care, as already mentioned in the introduction.

Self-advocacy, patient centricity, and patient empowerment are not just buzzwords; they are lifelines that help me, along with many others, steer through the challenges of managing our medical conditions—every day.

Luckily, if we fast forward to four decades later, I'm alive, and we live in a world that is smarter, more connected, and more patient friendly. A VBHC world where the best outcomes for patients, at the lowest cost for the system, are slowly emerging. However, much is still to be improved.

Let's take it step-by-step.

SELF-ADVOCACY, PATIENT CENTRICITY, PATIENT EMPOWERMENT: SAME, SAME, BUT DIFFERENT?

Understanding the differences between self-advocacy, patient centricity, and patient empowerment is critical in the journey toward better health outcomes (figure 1.2). These three key concepts have the potential to fundamentally create a more effective and patient-friendly healthcare system. This is how we understand them:

- *self-advocacy* leads to immediate actions and communication;
- *patient centricity* fosters a patient-focused health care environment; and
- *patient empowerment* builds sustained confidence and ability to manage health.

Figure 1.2: Three powerful concepts: self-advocacy, patient centricity, and patient empowerment.

Self-Advocacy	Actively participating in one's own health care by expressing needs, preferences, and concerns. ➢ It's the patient's voice in action - asking questions, seeking (second) opinions, and making informed decisions.
Patient Centricity	The healthcare system's commitment to design and deliver care that is centered around the patient's needs, values, and preferences. ➢ It's about creating a healthcare environment that listens to and respects the patient's voice.
Patient Empowerment	Enabling patients to take control of their health through knowledge, skills, and confidence as health literacy is to the benefit of each patient and an untapped resource for the system. ➢ It's about building the capacity for patients to manage their health proactively and effectively.

Under pressure to accept the stiff norms of diabetes care, as they were propagated by one-size-fits-all guidelines until recently, I felt unreasonable disease management expectations with only limited tools available. In the past, I felt like I had to avoid speaking up to doctors in a system that didn't expect a self-informed patient to ask any questions. It felt like a game governed by sticks and carrots, with incentives and outcomes dictated by doctors, and documents and diaries telling me what to eat and when to work out—yet, definitely not in a personalized manner. This was coupled with what felt like threats of worst-case scenarios in the form of complications—such as severe damage to my kidneys, eyes, and other vital organs. A terrifying scenario that dampens any chance of self-empowerment or, more specifically, *patient empowerment*. I went on to passively play the game, and, as a result, I simply stayed silent about living with diabetes.

That is, until my last trip to the ER. Exhausted and with no will to keep going like that, I made a decision. Once I started figuring out other ways and found other support networks to help me feel better, looking more closely at which kind of nutrition, sports, and insulins suited me, my lifestyle, and my condition the best, I started to slowly understand the connections better. (I was yet to understand the profound impact certain other lifestyle measures would have on my well-being, but more on that a little later.) Once I gained more confidence in my own care, I dared to become more vocal about living life with a chronic condition, caused by my very own immune system failing me. As the meme goes, "I'm so alpha that I kicked out my beta cells!" It's an exciting time for me to see more and more ways, tools, and measures on how to turn that ship around into more shallow waters of *patient centricity*. More proactive, partnering stands toward co-creating plans that work for me, my hobbies, my likings, and my lifestyle. And "carrots" that change outcomes to what matters to patients. All while the majority of my care was, and still is, managed outside of the healthcare system—"health happens at home."[1]

*I realized with time that by openly sharing my
own experiences and vulnerabilities, I am helping
others to better understand patients' realities.*

Today, I'm an expert patient leader, holding a MSc in diabetes from the University of Leicester, one of the world's top diabetes research centers, and working as a patient empowerment consultant. I am traveling the world as an international keynote speaker, sharing my story, as well as relevant research in the field, and growing my impact as part of several committees and boards—all to help people who happen to be patients to live better lives, including strengthening their *self-advocacy*.

This is something I certainly did not have on the bingo scorecard for my life!

THE IMPORTANCE OF
SELF-ADVOCACY IN HEALTH CARE

As Verena previously stated, "*patients are expecting health care on demand and want a trustworthy and empathetic provider-doctor relationship in which doctors listen to their needs and tailor care accordingly.*"[1] This hasn't changed. And it shouldn't be too much to ask for, either.

Self-advocacy is not just important—it's essential.

Imagine seeing a new doctor for a cut that got infected. Standard care protocol states to prescribe antibiotics, to which you are allergic. Time to speak up! Self-advocacy encourages open communication with providers, leading to more personalized and effective care, meaning you get medications that you tolerate, for example. It empowers patients to seek information, make informed decisions, and actively participate in their treatment plans. By advocating for ourselves, we ensure that our unique needs and values are respected and addressed. And, with seventy-five per cent of all deaths projected to be due to non-communicative (chronic) conditions in 2030, more of us will need to advocate and communicate our needs for our health, and find novel partnerships to create the right solutions for the right patients.[24] That's what we mean by outcomes that matter to patients, individually, and as a population.

The increasing digitalization of health care is a chance for everyone to further amplify self-advocacy and thereby improve care. It's all about connection. As Verena described in detail in the 'digital chapter' of her first book, when it comes to digitalization, health care has generally been quite late to the party, with certain exceptions to the rule.[1] For example, if you can provide more context around your health, with data from, say, your wearables, this is much better than turning to "Doctor Google—the all-knowing" for ideas or even (gasp!) a do-it-yourself diagnosis. Imagine if you could see a correlation between your new symptoms and your sleep quality trending down, or your resting heart rate being higher. Or, as someone living with Parkinson's disease, using the step counter on the smart watch to monitor gait. All are real signs that your body is dealing with something it usually doesn't and that could be worth further investigation. While we can certainly still discuss the role of artificial intelligence (AI) within health care, research shows that it can even help doctors to become more empathic in their communication and relationships with patients.[25–27]

But self-advocacy isn't easy. It requires strength, resilience, a deep understanding of your own body and feelings, and basic knowledge about your condition. Beyond that, we need to upskill in areas like medical and digital literacy, leadership, care coordination, effective collaboration, healthcare systems, and negotiation (don't miss Suzanne and Verena's chapter on this!). It requires a mindset that accepts and embraces the reality of our condition, leading to a clearer understanding of what we need to advocate for.

Ultimately, although daunting at first, no one is coming to save you, no one understands you as well as you want them to, no one can be there for you all the time—only you are responsible for your health and happiness.

Self-advocating can take a tremendous toll on your mental health. As if living with a health condition isn't difficult enough already, with worries about the past, present, and future! Although COVID-19 improved some aspects, I still feel that mental health is a necessary area of conversation in the health care field, especially when it comes to chronic care. Yet, part of the solution has already been mentioned in this book—self-care and treating yourself to stay motivated, whether that means buying a new handbag or taking a break (perhaps on the beach?). It's to acknowledge in the short term your own hard work as the master of your own health, and to avoid burnout in the long run.

Make sure you look out for *number one* first!

Figure 1.3: Self-care: be your own number one.

If you muster up the courage and strength to "be your own best doctor" as a patient, the least that should be expected is for your doctor to show up in the same way. Together, based on a relationship built on trust, understanding, and equality, you can move mountains in the health care world. And you need that "ally" on your side to do so; without them, you have no care at all.

A HOLISTIC APPROACH TO HEALTH

Taking good care of yourself as a patient goes far beyond taking your pills and injections, moving your body, and possibly eating "right." It's truly time to step up your game and realize that health and well-being is a holistic matter. In a manner of speaking, we need to befriend our companions, especially the ones we haven't chosen ourselves (like a health condition) and understand as much as we can about them. We certainly can't afford to leave our health leaning on the sometimes rigid education in a one-size-fits-all system. You will read more about VBHC as an opportunity to tailor health care more to the individual in Chapter 4.

Figure 1.4: The six dimensions in the Wheel of Health.

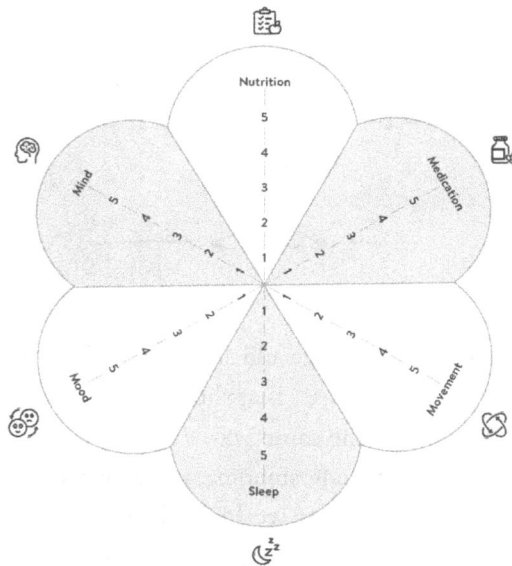

© 5P Health Care Solutions – 5PEP program

We need to be able to live our lives to the fullest, with and *despite* whatever condition it is that labels us as *patients*, and aim at gaining partnerships around us that fuel our sense of *self-care*, all in order to bring more *care* into health care.

Working along the six dimensions in the Wheel of Health has had the most impact on me. And it hasn't just been an n=1 experiment! What later became the 5PEP (Patient Empowerment Program) at 5P Health Care Solutions has been a cornerstone in my own journey toward balanced self-care, and became an integral part to my coaching work with patients and groups in workshops.[28]

As illustrated in figure 1.4, the Wheel of Health emphasizes the importance of a balanced approach across six mainstays of health: nutrition, medication, movement, sleep, mood, and mind.

By focusing on these dimensions, I can create a more holistic approach to my well-being. I invite anyone curious about novel ways to impact their own health to try this out. For example, I've come to realize that a blanket statement such as "Eat what you want and just take insulin for it" doesn't quite apply to me. I've found much better long-term results in focusing my nutrition on protein and fibrous vegetables—and leaving rice, bread, and pasta to those who can handle them better. Finding my own way to better, more sustainable ways of regular movement has also been key, instead of running or going to the gym (yawn!). Same rule applies to finding my own sleep rhythm and patterns, which is a huge factor in blood glucose management. And finding ways of taking better care of my mood and mind have helped me tremendously in many ways.

It's important that patients step up to the plate in literacy, empowerment, and advocacy to find ways that help integrate this powerful Wheel of Health—coupled with respective support such as coaches, apps, and communities—into their self-care program.

Before we move on, a quick word about the sixth dimension: medication. Essentially, yes, people living with different medical conditions very often need medication, some simply to stay alive— insulin for T1D or life-saving chemotherapy for cancer. But from a population-health perspective, we know that medication only contributes a mere eleven per cent to overall health outcomes. At least forty per cent can be influenced by our own behaviors and lifestyle choices![1]

There is simply so much more that we can do ourselves to improve our health outside of the doctor's office.

In my earliest conversations with Verena, we concluded that *"self-empowered patients, and choosing options 'beyond the pill' are an untapped potential on the way to value creation."*[1] Achieving this balance ain't easy. These six dimensions aren't a mirror-image of the reality of living with a condition that never takes a break, either. Sorry about that! The truth is, while self-care and a holistic mindset are vital, they should be supported by a healthcare system that is streamlined, efficient, and responsive to individual patient needs. Useless bureaucracy, lack of support, and systemic inefficiencies can make it difficult for patients, providers, and others to actually focus on outcomes that matter.

The 5PEP program brings the Wheel of Health into a structured nine-week coaching program and deploys a dual chance for impact. It serves both the patients and the system, as self-empowerment through health literacy was shown to directly improve health outcomes that matter! [29] In other words, while self-care certainly is a personal responsibility, the healthcare system also has a crucial role to play in supporting that journey. It is about giving patients the tools and support they need—and removing the barriers that prevent them from fully participating in their own care. All five actors dancing the tango in health care have a role to play to reap the best possible benefits.

THE ROLE OF THE HEALTHCARE SYSTEM: SUPPORTING SELF-ADVOCACY AND EMPOWERMENT

Patients cannot navigate this journey alone. Nor should they.

As mentioned in the introduction, as patients, we all need a medical dream team, a support system that includes health care providers, patient advocates, support groups, as well as family and friends. Each of these stakeholders plays a crucial role in helping patients advocate for themselves and manage their health effectively. For me, my medical dream team is based on working with providers that help me realize health goals that we set in co-creation. This is a big roundtable due to the complexity of the condition, comprised of a GP, an endocrinologist, a podiatrist, an ophthalmologist, a psychiatrist, a nurse, a phlebotomist, along with various "by demand" specialists for checkups every couple of years, such as a cardiologist, a thyroid specialist, a kidney specialist, a dietician, a personal trainer, and a dermatologist. Phew!

The point is: care coordination is a big thing, and can certainly be helped by the digitalization of care and instant sharing of data to get these actors to work better together! It also requires the human touch; you need to find the right match for you, with a willingness from both patient and provider to collaborate—chemistry needs to be present both ways. In fact, the care professionals that I remember the fondest have all displayed one simple, highly intra-personal trait: they were able to listen to me, and take my concerns and my goals seriously, with empathy and understanding that while my condition is a part of me, it's not *all* of me. We just need to clone them (or teach the rest how it's done)!

I welcome the new trend of pulling back the curtain on hierarchical, old-school, one-size-fits-all medicine in favor of collaborative, participatory engagement between partners.

Arguably, as the doctor-patient relationship is the backbone of healthcare, providers must build strong, communicative relationships with their patients, ensuring that concerns and preferences are heard and addressed. As with any relationship, you need to cultivate a sense of trust. This may not be possible within seven-minute slots (rendered by a useless RVU system!) and delivered in three visits a year (not enough to reflect my 24/7/365 reality!). Hence both Verena and I often state, *"What doctors and nurses want is more time: more quality time spent with the patient, and less time wasted with bureaucracy!"*[1] In addition to time, building trust requires showing vulnerability, harnessing strengths, standing for your values, and meeting the other as your equal. Engagements in *real-talk* and encounters as humans! What becomes increasingly important in this particular relationship is that language does matter. Born from the Diabetes Online Community (DOC), the

"Language Matters!" position paper emphasizes the importance of using appropriate and sensitive language when discussing diabetes, focusing on the impact of words on individuals' self-esteem, motivation, and mental health, and advocating for person-centered language to communicate without blame or stigma. This encourages empowerment, and fosters a collaborative relationship between HCPs and individuals living with diabetes.[27] Essentially, understanding each other's needs, problems, and feelings is how we move toward our collective goal.

The challenge of how to get started is surprisingly human! It begins with listening.

Listen, ask, learn, ask, do—repeat!

Intensifying interactions with patients, advocacy groups, and others comes with a big warning sign; it can never become simply a check-box activity. As much as I welcome the plethora of VBHC initiatives, we need to be mindful of the quality.[30, 31] If not put into the right context, purpose, and framework, they become exactly that: check-boxing the number of SOPs (standard operating procedures) developed, QIs (quality indicators) met, and forms sent back to the government (more on that in Chapter 4).

While more healthy competition and market disruptors are available in the pharmaceutical landscape, the patient voice needs to be further strengthened. Whereas several pharmaceutical companies do collaborate with patient organizations and some even truly co-create their solutions together with patients (eureka!), as you will see in later chapters, there is a need for more organizations to do more. If you are able to include the patient voice in your work as one of the other four actors in the 5P value chain, make sure to consistently consult with patient representatives, compensate them for their time and expertise, and hold yourself accountable for creating a solution or medicine that actually *solves* the patients' problem—please!

This is where standardized tools can come in to enable further insights into the patients' experience, well-being and personal goals.

Tools such as patient-reported outcome measures (PROMs) and patient-reported experience measures (PREMs), along with their clinician counterpart—clinician-reported outcome measures (CROMs), can enhance person-centricity within health care and look to both clinical outcomes and societal factors such as social determinants of health (SDOH).

Figure 1.5: The interplay of PROMs and PREMs and how they come together beautifully.

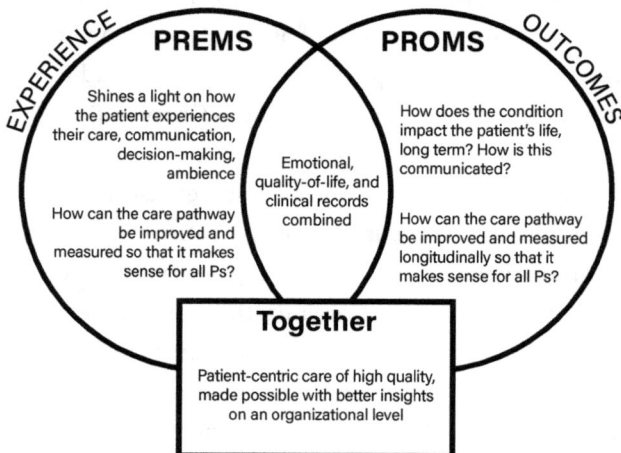

EXPERIENCE

PREMS

Shines a light on how the patient experiences their care, communication, decision-making, ambience

How can the care pathway be improved and measured so that it makes sense for all Ps?

Emotional, quality-of-life, and clinical records combined

PROMS

OUTCOMES

How does the condition impact the patient's life, long term? How is this communicated?

How can the care pathway be improved and measured longitudinally so that it makes sense for all Ps?

Together

Patient-centric care of high quality, made possible with better insights on an organizational level

As showcased in figure 1.5, these tools enhance patient empowerment and self-advocacy, person-centric care, and informed decision making; support continuous self-management; and create a feedback loop and ultimately system improvement. Together, they build a foundation for person-centered, holistic care that honors patient voices, enhances patient agency, and fosters meaningful partnerships between patients and clinicians.

What if there was a roadmap to get all these steps in this giant tango together? One idea would be to start with the "three steps to VBHC", depicted in figure 1.6.

In brief, define whom you want to help (the medical condition), followed by what you want to achieve in co-creation with them and what matters to the patient population (the outcome), ending with what actors are needed to solve the problems that the patients are facing (the activities).

This journey requires several stakeholders, some of which you have already encountered in the aforementioned medical dream team for my condition (T1D). You will find out more in subsequent chapters (namely Chapter 4), including how they play into the choreography of the tango of patient centricity.

Figure 1.6: Three steps to VBHC: focusing on the shared needs of patients with one medical condition, defining the desired outcomes together across the 5Ps, and aligning the actors and activities required to achieve these outcomes are the core ingredients of Value-Based Health Care.

© 5P Health Care Solutions

THE STARFISH STORY: THE POWER OF SMALL STEPS

Empowering yourself as a patient is a powerful step to take. Along with educational responsibilities, another challenge of patient empowerment is the relatively small n=1 impact, illustrating the idea that individual actions may seem insignificant in the larger picture.

I promised you I'd get back to the beach analogy for self-care. The starfish story reminds us that every small step matters.[33]

STARFISH ON THE BEACH

An old man had a habit of early morning walks on the beach.

One day, after a storm, he saw a human figure in the distance moving like a dancer. As he came closer, he saw that it was a young woman and she was not dancing but was reaching down to the sand, picking up starfish and very gently throwing them into the ocean.

"Young lady," he asked, "why are you throwing starfish into the ocean?"

"The sun is up, and the tide is going out, and if I do not throw them in, they will die."

"But young lady, do you not realize that there are miles and miles of beach and starfish all along it? You cannot possibly make a difference."

The young woman listened politely, paused and then bent down, picked up another starfish and threw it into the sea, past the breaking waves, before saying, "It made a difference for that one."

Talking of small steps, and choosing which starfish get thrown back into the ocean, makes me think of the patient stratification required in tailoring care plans to groups of patients with similar needs. As you have seen in figure 1.6, much of our efforts in VBHC lie in getting more specific care to a patient population living with one medical condition, just like I do with T1D in the various steps of my life, as a kid, a teenager, or a young woman. Remember my callout for the waste of money and efforts with one-size-fits-all approaches that don't work? Imagine if we could take one "starfish" at a time—for each group of patients sharing similar needs and co-create tailored solutions for exactly each group. That would have been ideal for me as a teenager, for example!

The reality is: although navigating the ocean of health care can be rough seas, one patient advocating for their health can inspire others to do the same, creating a ripple effect that leads to broader systemic change. Telling your story and sharing your experiences is powerful, as it catalyzes others to do the same and motivates those who are in a different point of their patient journey, just like the opening quote for this chapter says. Sharing unites you.

Lastly, like a well-choreographed tango, another step is the power of community playing a key role, for several reasons.

Let me share five critical reasons why I strongly believe in the power of community and peer support—especially when living with a condition that is always at the back of your mind 24/7/365.

Firstly, for emotional support. Living with a chronic condition can be overwhelming, so being part of a community helps individuals connect with others who truly understand their experiences, providing a sense of belonging and emotional relief. For example, it is easy to seek support in the diabetes online community when something unexpected happens (which it does in life with diabetes—it likes to keep us on our toes!), and we *know* most of the community has been through something similar at one point or another.

Secondly, shared knowledge. Communities offer a platform to share advice, tips, and personal experiences about managing the condition. This collective wisdom can help individuals discover new coping strategies, treatments, and lifestyle adaptations, among other things.

Thirdly, communities provide accountability and motivation to keep going. When surrounded by others with similar challenges, people often feel more motivated to stick to their health routines, whether it's following treatment plans, maintaining a healthy diet, or exercising.

Fourthly, feeling less alone. Chronic diseases can sometimes make people feel isolated, especially if their condition limits their activities. Being part of a supportive group helps reduce loneliness, and enhances a sense of connection and normalcy.

Finally, being part of a community enables advocacy and empowerment. Communities often unite people to raise awareness, push for better healthcare policies, or fund research. This collective effort can lead to tangible improvements in health care and inspire individuals to feel empowered in their own care journey.

BUILDING A PATIENT-CENTRIC FUTURE

Amid recent trends and developments within health care—such as the VBHC movement with its focus on rewarding and paying for outcomes—it is clear to me that individualization of care, which makes sense to the patient, aligns with their health goals, and facilitates collaboration at an eye-to-eye level, is within reach. Preserving health today and reducing disease progression tomorrow in a truly holistic framework with outcomes that really matter. This means that we, as patients, need to be the main focus of the equation.

As a patient, I have learned that self-advocacy, patient centricity, and patient empowerment are not just nice-to-have concepts—they are the keys to navigating the complex world of health care. But for these efforts to be truly effective, they must be supported by a healthcare system that listens, respects, and empowers patients. It's always a two-way, no, a five-way street!

While living with type 1 diabetes looks very different today in comparison to when I was a child, in terms of technology, tools, and medications available, health care as a whole doesn't seem to have followed suit to the same extent. The journey toward a value-based, patient-centric healthcare system is not just about individual actions; it's about collective efforts. It's about creating a health care environment where patients are at the center, where their voices are heard, and where their empowerment is supported every step of the way. Sounds so simple, right? Then, why is it so difficult? Are we there yet? We are about to find out in the upcoming chapters.

In this journey, I am not alone. I am part of a broader community of patients, advocates, providers, payers, pharma, and policymakers who are working together to build a better, more patient-centric future.

The great news with a VBHC model is that patient centricity is at, well, the center. This requires the other 4P to collaborate with patients. Specifically, for the providers to listen and understand everyday life (and I particularly welcome the next chapter about participative provider research!), for pharma to develop solutions that work, for payers to keep an open mind about the fact that health care, at large, is individual, and for policymakers to enable and empower patients to come together in a beautifully choreographed tango of health care.

☆ PATIENT REFLECTION BOX
ON THE WHEEL OF HEALTH

Remember the Wheel of Health we discussed earlier? Before we move on, here are some questions to consider in relation to the six dimensions.

- **Nutrition:** What is one small, positive change I can make to my eating habits today that will support my health and energy? Do I need coaching on this?

- **Medication:** Do I fully understand how my medications work and how they fit into my overall treatment plan? Do I have the right care team?

- **Movement:** How can I incorporate movement into my day in a way that feels enjoyable and aligns with my physical abilities?

- **Sleep:** What steps can I take tonight to create a sleep routine that helps me feel more rested and energized tomorrow?

- **Mood:** How can I check in with myself regularly to recognize and address my emotions, so I feel more balanced and in control?

- **Mind:** What practices, like mindfulness or relaxation techniques, can I try to manage stress and improve my mental clarity? Who can I ask for support about my own self-advocacy as a patient?

CHAPTER 2

The *Provider* view on the role of participative research for value creation

By Claudia Canella and Claudia Witt

*"Vulnerability is the birthplace of inno-
vation, creativity, and change."*

~ BRENÉ BROWN

When Hanna and Verena first approached us to collaborate on this *Next Tango*, it didn't take us long to agree and join what looks like a great set of co-authors!

Indeed, most people would intuitively agree that it is favorable when people with different backgrounds, who are affected by a certain illness or medical condition (such as cancer, diabetes, or multiple sclerosis), would come together and collaborate both in regular care delivery as well as in health research about the health issue in question. But how to actually do it? And, what can this look like in reality? This is where our academic focus of *participative research* comes into play. Both the necessity to share interests and needs, as well as a look beyond the curtain of a traditional doctor-patient relationship into a *TangoForFive*, resonates deeply with what we do in our day jobs at the center of integrative and complementary medicine at the University of Zurich.

Our aim here is to shed some light and insights on how participative research gets in sync with the tango of patient centricity.

By reading this chapter, you will be able to get a "first steps" guide in case you're interested in planning or participating in a medical participatory research project yourself. It is also intended to build a bridge between academic methodological knowledge and practical experience, and demonstrate the range of possible approaches and different objectives within our area of research in medicine. Lastly, of course, we'd like to showcase the impact of bringing participation from research to real-life care delivery and engage in a dialogue with you, the reader, and participate in that tango.

Ready to learn from some of our real-life, practical experiences?

Let's continue the dance!

IT TAKES TWO CLAUDIAS TO TANGO: PROVIDERS IN DIALOGUE

Once we had hung up the phone with Hanna and Verena, we went into this very first brainstorming dialogue among ourselves. Listen to this...

Claudia C.: "Claudia W., we have practiced the tango of five for ten years together in a specific area of medical research that informs real-life clinical care. Similar to the tango as a dance genre, you and I approached it slowly and gently, then getting more playful and experimental along the dance and with different projects over the years.

An experience of a recent study that stays in my heart is co-creating a digital mind-body medicine intervention with people living with amyotrophic lateral sclerosis (ALS). It showed me how far we are able to go with inclusion and participation in research as we worked together with people affected by ALS of a very broad spectrum concerning their constraints. Half of the participants had almost no constraints while the other half had disabilities such as paralysis, limited speaking abilities, and, in one case, a person near a locked-in state, what means complete paralysis with the exception of the ability to move the eyes.

Now, here in this book, I am motivated to share our experiences with the tango of five based on concrete participatory digital health research projects.

It seems important to me to put research in integrative medicine at the service of people who have to cope with their individual health condition every day.

And on the other side, to utilize the patient's expertise by experience for the benefit of researchers to make it even more relevant. Thus, ultimately fostering the implementation of participatory approaches into routine care and everyday life for patients and providers.

How about you, Claudia W.?"

Claudia W.: "It makes me happy that you describe our approach in Zurich as playful and experimental, especially in the relation to dance—this is exactly what I aimed to achieve. When I first started stakeholder engagement in clinical trials twenty years ago, the process was much more rigid and top-down—similar to the description of Hanna's experience. At that time, we were planning a study on acupressure and mindfulness exercises for young women experiencing menstrual pain, using more old-fashioned methods like paper questionnaires and one-way interviews.

What I quickly had to learn was a bit of a bummer for me. 'My' stakeholders didn't like the idea of my research as much as I seemed to at the time. Do you know why? Well, first, I had to drop the mindfulness intervention that I had added as a second intervention to make it a bit more 'modern' (and something I was personally interested in!) because the young women made it clear to me that they didn't want to meditate (this was twenty years ago!). Second, and in hindsight that was encouraging, they expressed a preference for an app to guide the acupressure intervention.

Though it was difficult to digest at the time, this experience marked a positive turning point in my career and approach to research. It pushed me into digital health research with apps much earlier than I had anticipated, and stakeholder engagement became an integral part of all my projects.

———————————

Over the years, I've expanded my (digital) toolbox and gained broader experience, which I now refer to as participatory research methods.

———————————

I take great pride in sharing these insights with others who are motivated to explore this path. It is only by involving all five actors in the tango in a collaborative fashion that we can truly reap broad value creation for all stakeholders. The field of participatory research is a perfect match toward this goal. But it is also quite complex, which is why I value the opportunity to provide systematic guidance in this book, enriched with real-world case studies from our work."

So, in conclusion from our own first dialogue, we decided that throughout this chapter, running under the title of "provider view," we'd like to take a *participative* approach with you. As we share three real-life cases, we invite you to draw on your own experiences and reflect on how you can relate or not relate to the experiences described. We ask two main questions:

- Which personal experiences brought you to *The Next Tango*?
- What are your values or hopes for participation in research?

WHEN THE FIVE TANGO TOGETHER IN HEALTH RESEARCH, WE CALL IT PARTICIPATORY RESEARCH

When patients, providers, pharma, payers, and policy tango together in health care, be it in R&D or in regular care delivery, we refer to it as participatory. In our specific field of academic expertise in integrative and complementary medicine, we therefore call it *participatory research* with the aim of fostering better collaborative care delivery models, which Hanna calls for loud and clear in the previous chapter.

Similarly to the three-step process of VBHC, showcased in figure 1.6, it is not our preference to talk about diseases or illnesses, or, worse, even put patients in buckets such as "the diabetic patient" or "the cancer patient." Rather, we aim to make it more participatory. Instead of "illness" and "disease," we more neutrally refer to it as *health issues* because not every condition necessarily makes people feel sick, such as a small infected skin scratch or a woman with an uncomplicated pregnancy. The conclusion: talking about health, rather than fostering sickness. This is the approach we are taking by focusing holistically on the entire health continuum.

So, who takes part in our research?

People affected by various conditions and health issues stemming from a variety of different origins and therapeutic areas. We stand strong to say that people in clinical trials and research projects are neither *subjects* nor necessarily *patients* (such as, for example, studies for new products in healthy volunteers.)

Words. Do. Matter. We say: people are not merely recipients nor donors of clinical trials.

The goal is to conduct research projects WITH the people, rather than FOR or about them.

We fully recognize people's lived experiences and priorities on a 24/7 basis as our primary goal.[34-37] As much as we refer to people rather than patients, we also refer to the five main actors more generically as *stakeholders in health research*. Therefore, bear with us as we are applying this terminology throughout this chapter. The scope of stakeholders we interact with is very broad. They come with backgrounds such as:

- A patient living with a condition impacting their daily living or their survival prognosis, or more broadly someone living with a condition who may be asymptomatic but requiring treatment. In both instances, we refer to them as a person directly affected by a health issue.
- A family member, caregiver, or a friend of a person indirectly affected by a health issue.
- People representing a health profession that is involved in the treatment of the health issue in question, such as medical doctors, nurse experts, physiotherapists, psychologists, integrative medicine health professionals, dieticians, etc.
- People from the public sector, such as researchers, policymakers, health insurers, the pharmaceutical industry, and patient advocacy organizations.[34, 37, 46]

Participatory approaches aim to be inclusive and ensure that research findings are not only shared within the scientific community but are also applied in the real-world care setting.

In our participatory projects, there can be varying levels of stakeholder involvement, from lower degrees of barely informational and contributory participation to higher levels such as collaborative, co-creative, or co-leading roles (figure 2.1).

Figure 2.1: Levels of participation, stages of involvement in the research process, involved sectors, and role types of stakeholders.[37]

LEVELS OF PARTICIPATION	STAGES OF INVOLVEMENT	SECTORS	ROLE TYPES
Information	Identification of needs	Private: patients, family, friends, caregivers	Personal engagement
Contribution			
Consultation	Priorities of research		HCP
		HCPs: doctors, nurses, physio-therapists	Adviser
Co-creation	Study design & documents		Expert
Partnership			
Co-lead	Methods development	Public: researchers, policy, pharma, patient advocate organizations	Co-researcher
	Recruitment		
	Data collection & analysis		
	Validation & implementation		
	Publication		

The level of engagement chosen depends as much on the research goals, with each degree being equally valuable based on the context, as on the willingness and interest of stakeholders, such as patients and families, to contribute more or less. Formats may involve stakeholders sharing their experiences and priorities through interviews, focus groups, or surveys.[37, 38, 46] Meanwhile, higher levels of participation, like collaborative or co-leading approaches, involve stakeholders in every phase of the research process, from planning to implementation and communication.

Our foundational methods often include traditional tools such as structured interviews, questionnaires, and surveys. Additionally, due to the collaborative nature of our research, stakeholders also participate in creative and interactive approaches such as work-shops, arts-based methods, or design thinking sessions, all fueled by modern digital apps and communication channels. It allows for smarter and deeper engagement throughout the research. The roles of stakeholders can vary widely, from providing personal insights as individuals affected by a health issue to serving as experts representing advocacy organizations or even acting as co-researchers.[37, 38, 46]

To bring these theoretical considerations to life, we are sharing three real-life use cases of participatory digital health research projects. They were all conducted at our institution of com-plementary and integrative medicine in Zurich. They include evidence-based complementary medicine practices, therapies, digital health measures, or products that are used in tight coor-dination with conventional medicine.[47, 48]

MAKING IT REAL: APPLYING PARTICIPATIVE RESEARCH FOR BETTER PATIENT OUTCOMES

Our use cases cover three diverse health issues:

- Cancer,
- Multiple sclerosis (MS), and
- Amyotrophic lateral sclerosis (ALS).

Firstly, the DITRAS project was conceived to provide digital train-ing support to persons living with cancer so they could eventually apply self-care methods, just like Hanna and Verena call for in the introductory and patient chapters earlier.[49] The project develops interventions and related eLearning tools that support patients to use self-care methods such as acupressure and mindfulness. Along the veins of the Wheel of Health (figure 1.4), these self-care measures aim to positively impact sleep, fatigue, and treatment-related nausea and vomiting. A standardized framework will help determine patient preferences for a certain method. The main participative research focus comprises the development of a digital tool and deploying a variety of communication channels to reach a broad spectrum of patients and stakeholders affected by cancer.

Secondly, the PEMS project studies the participatory evidence of complementary medicine in multiple sclerosis.[50] It identifies priorities expressed by patients and relevant stakeholders affected by MS in Switzerland relating to complementary medicine approaches and therapies. Importantly, and following the three-step VBHC process that Hanna describes in Chapter 1, the overall objective of this project is also to develop a core outcome set to demonstrate the impact that complementary medicine can have for MS. The particular participatory focus lies in the cooperation among all stakeholders and institutions such as patient organizations and the Cochrane Collaboration.[51] As an output of this project, the prioritization of patient-related outcomes and the respective supportive studies are depicted and visualized through an online evidence and gap map.

Lastly, the RIMA initiative investigates resource-oriented integrative methods for people with ALS.[52] It answers this question: Which kind of digital complementary and integrative medicine support (i.e. an app-guided breathing exercise or a telephone consultation) are considered supportive and which settings are needed to incorporate them into everyday life (i.e. clinic, telcare, eLearnings)? As its main participative focus, this project works through the co-creation of a digital intervention by the researchers with its end-users, (i.e. patients and family), while making the end product as individual- and user-friendly as possible.

Figure 2.2 provides an overview of the sectors and stakeholders involved in these three projects. It covers their level of participation, role types, and stages of involvement.

Figure 2.2: Sectors and stakeholders involved in the three use case projects, levels of participation, stages of involvement, and role types.

Use Case Project	Sectors & Stakeholders	Levels of participation	Stages of involvement	Role types
DITRAS	√ PRIVATE: cancer patients √ HCPs: oncologists, nurses, psychologists, TCM, MBM √ PUBLIC: researchers, experts in education √ OTHER: Stakeholder Advisory Board	√ Information √ Contribution √ Consultation √ Collaboration	√ Identification of needs √ Prioritization of research topics √ Study design & documents √ Methods development √ Recruitment √ Validation of results √ Publication, Co-authorship	√ Personal engagement √ Professional √ Advisor √ Expert
PEMS	√ PRIVATE: people with MS, friends and family, caregivers √ HCPs: neurologists, nurses, integrative medicine √ PUBLIC: researchers √ OTHER: Stakeholder Advisory Board	√ Information √ Contribution √ Consultation √ Collaboration	√ Identification of needs √ Prioritization of research topics √ Study protocol documents √ Recruitment √ Validation of results √ Publication, Co-authorship √ Implementation	√ Personal engagement √ Professional √ Advisor √ Expert
RIMA	√ PRIVATE: people with ALS √ HCPs: neurologists, integrative medicine, MBM √ PUBLIC: Researchers, ALS patient organizations	√ Information √ Contribution √ Consultation √ Collaboration √ Co-creation	√ Identification of needs √ Study design & documents √ Methods development √ Recruitment √ Validation of results √ Implementation	√ Personal engagement √ Professional √ Advisor √ Expert

In the following parts of this chapter, we highlight six critical dimensions that govern the success of participative research, bringing it to life each time with examples stemming from these three use case projects.

Ready?

POTENTIALS AND CHALLENGES
FOR A TANGO OF FIVE

Like any approach, we are faced with pitfalls and opportunities in this particular set of research in integrative medicine. To make the most of it and put all odds on best success, here is our conclusion for six areas of governance to make participative research results impactful in daily life.

1. Participation

The most powerful thing about participatory research is that people affected by a health issue get involved.[34-45] That sounds trivial, doesn't it? However, the devil lies in the details of implementation. We are talking not only of the patient who of course is front and center. But we also approach it holistically throughout the value chain of five actors. The difficulty here being how to ensure that diversity is considered and key players are on board. One of the most important first steps is to identify the key stakeholders relevant for each condition—just as Hanna refers to the three-step process of VBHC, being specific of the disease area, health issue, or medical condition makes the difference to bring real impactful solutions to people. As a consequence, the required actors need to get involved to achieve specific outcomes in this population. In DITRAS, for example, the spectrum of actors is as large as: patients who had or were having anti-cancer treatment, such as chemotherapy, radiotherapy, or immunotherapy; oncologists, cancer nurse experts, Traditional Chinese Medicine (TCM) specialists, mind-body medicine specialists; and psychologists, researchers, and eLearning education experts.

We often form a stakeholder advisory board in our projects to ensure key stakeholders are involved in every stage of the research and the decision making.

In PEMS, we collaborate with well-established institutions, such as the Cochrane Collaboration regarding the research methods, and the Swiss MS Society as an important advocacy organization.[51, 53] These collaborations allowed us to reach around 1,700 people affected by MS and other stakeholders, and integrate their views and priorities.

Research that informs routine care usually aims to provide an intervention that preferably is useful for a broad range of people affected by the given health issue. This also means that we should aim to involve people with a diversity of: origin, age, gender, socio-economic status, educational background, and a variety of clinical conditions.[34-45]

Figure 2.3: Stakeholder advisory group.

2. Accessibility

Fostering participation also means thinking about accessibility, such as barrier-free access to clinics. More specifically: people's distance from home to reach the hospital or institution where the research project is taking place. And, accounting for underserved areas and populations who still may be lacking fast-speed internet cable connections. It is important to consider these practicalities, such as the example of transportation vouchers linked to outcomes, as Verena has described them previously from the Oak Street Health organization in the US Midwest.[1] In RIMA, we individually discussed with each participant their accessibility needs and preferences. It led to the conclusion to conduct meetings and workshops online, and to co-create an online mind-body intervention, as this setting best fitted their accessibility needs and preferences. Digital health projects and interventions often offer barrier-adaptable, open-access solutions that people can utilize from their homes (health happens at home!), meaning they do not need to travel or be in environments that they feel less comfortable in, like hospitals. Stakeholders in RIMA or DITRAS provided feedback that eLearning modules are preferable for them, because they can integrate them perfectly in their everyday life, like when their kids are at school or when they usually have the most energy, as fatigue is often a big problem for patients dealing with cancer, MS or ALS.

3. Human and financial resources

Two big challenges for the success of participatory research are human and financial resources to fund these projects. Financing is a central subject in this book, and the following chapters are entirely dedicated to this complex topic of paying for care and research in medicine. Hence, it is critical to think about how to organize and run participative processes in order to bring them to fruition and not bounce off the hurdle of who will actually pay for it. We need to consider things like infrastructure, time constraints, and the allocation of human and financial resources. These can be tricky to navigate, particularly when we're dealing with diverse and complex health-related restrictions, and diversity among stakeholders.[34-45] In recent years, especially since COVID-19, there has been increasing pressure for medical research to find quick solutions to health issues. Research timelines are getting shorter, but funding is not keeping up, which puts a strain on the financial stability—as you will read in more detail in the following chapter. One common challenge is ensuring fair compensation for stakeholders who participate in research, as funds for this purpose are often limited. On top of that, people who get disability pensions sometimes have to make a tough choice: should they accept financial compensation for their time and effort, or risk losing some of their pension benefits?[34-45]

Until now, we have not found the perfect solution that fits all our projects. As a means of reward though, we always propose co-authorship in scientific publications to our participants if they fulfill certain criteria for co-authorship.[54] If we do have enough third-party funding, we ask the participants what type of compensation they prefer, whether it's money or vouchers or something else. Most often, we all have to accept a compromise. For example, in PEMS, we only had funding for the participating people with MS in the stakeholder advisory board. For the other stakeholders, such as HCPs and researchers, we were able to offer co-authorship in scientific publications.

*On the other hand, we know from participatory
research that the most common reason for
stakeholders to take part is the desire to contribute to
research so that future patients receive better care.*

Therefore, motivation seems to be more related to value creation
and feeling involved than to monetary incentives.

4. Shared language and conflicting interests

Singing from the same song sheet and dancing in a *TangoForFive*
means adopting a common vocabulary—speaking a "shared language." Both Hanna, in the preceding chapter, and Suzanne, in
the concluding chapter, refer to this loud and clear to allow all
actors to understand each other. To ensure this among all the
participating stakeholders in a complex multistakeholder project, this means being able to manage conflicting interests as an
additional challenge in participatory research.[34-45] The MPC song
sheet process of seven steps helps to bridge various interests into
one purpose and project goal—as nicely described by Suzanne
in that concluding chapter. The challenge we posed ourselves,
by choosing this vein of research, is dealing with a very diverse
group of stakeholders every time we design, conduct, and analyze
a participatory research project. We can't just assume that we are
all speaking the same language nor that our values and interests
align. In addition, health care professionals and researchers often
use a very technical and specialized language that is hard for the
general public to understand.

*It is therefore advisable to be aware of using a
common language, to invest in encounters at
eye level, and to address the topics explicitly
and repeatedly to bring everyone on board.*

Sometimes, the "sixth P" can be helpful. Done so in the RIMA project, where we hired an external process moderator to foster shared language and negotiate conflicting interests among the stakeholders. In PEMS, Claudia Canella herself, as a researcher specializing in participatory health research, took on the role of facilitator in the project. In DITRAS, Claudia Witt, with her long-term experience in engaging stakeholders in research, took the role of ensuring eye-to-eye-level discussions and fostering a common language. Dancing the tango to a common song sheet in real life!

5. Feasibility and implementation

The true power of participatory research is that you can get something practical and ready for implementation in regular care settings, such as an intervention, a tool, or a self-care method, because it aligns to the values and priorities of you and the people affected by a specific health issue.[34-45] However, it often needs prototyping, followed by a consecutive project to test and validate the clinical effectiveness and to accompany the rollout into the clinic. Our projects are good examples of this.

In RIMA, we co-created an online mind-body medicine exercise together with stakeholders affected by ALS and tested a prototype with them in our clinic. As outlined before, funding bottlenecks occur along the way. For this particular project, it took a while to secure additional funding to research the clinical effectiveness. In DITRAS, we first created an eLearning prototype together with stakeholders. And as a second step, with new funding, we further developed and validated the tool within a clinical trial for effectiveness. In PEMS, we created an online evidence and gap map displaying research studies that evaluate the effects of complementary therapies on specific outcomes for people with MS. Together with the advocacy organization MS Society Switzerland, we collaboratively worked on the distribution and implementation of this map.

6. Science communication

We already referred to the power of shared language. Further, bridging the gap between science talk and real-life doctor-patient talk is an additional challenge—and opportunity.

While there is a lot of good research out there, not many people know about it and often not the ones who are directly affected by the topic under study. This is a task for everyone involved, but certainly researchers carry a main responsibility to make research output more broadly understandable and involve lay audiences in the transcripts of what may read like a cryptic research report.[34-45] In a participatory research project, we should think carefully about whom we are mainly doing the research for, and how we can inform participants about what we are doing. To whom do the results really matter? The answer is: patients obtaining better outcomes for their health issue at hand!

In our projects, we are usually producing video abstracts for the general public and regularly post on our social media channels about the progress. We additionally work with the media department of our hospital and with the involved stakeholders, such as other hospitals or advocacy organizations, to broaden the reach of our information.

WHAT CAN WE LEARN FROM PARTICIPATORY RESEARCH FOR CLINICAL PRACTICE?

In order to put our approach of participative research into the broader context of the other 5P perspectives, there are a few points we wanted to raise awareness about. As much as the benefits may now be obvious to patients and providers, the payer and policy angles may be less straightforward. However, as Hanna and Verena have been asking us, "How does this research translate into real-world patient care?" To answer that question, we would like to raise the importance of funding and sustainability. For example, in the instance of the DITRAS project, we were able to secure collaborative funding to translate the research results into clinical practice for people living with cancer. On the contrary, patients with ALS in the RIMA project are not yet able to obtain this kind of proven benefit support in real-life care because of ongoing research funding bottlenecks. What other actors could contribute to make this a more sustainable value proposition? Is there a role for health insurers to become interested and involved (as you will read about in Chapter 4)? What about the pharmaceutical industry to co-create holistic support care initiatives into the real-life setting (we are glad to see at least one example flagged in the next chapter)? Policymakers could also become intrigued by the results of our participative research, as the effect on large-scale population health conditions may be very beneficial (projects listed in Chapter 5 provide a wide range of possible perspectives).

Finally, and as we are wrapping up this chapter on the provider perspective on participative research to achieve joint value creation and patient centricity, we are closing with another short dialogue.

Claudia C.: "When I think about how the experiences from our participative research project could be transferred to clinical health care practice, I envision topics of the *how and the method* as well as topics relating to *what and values*. Firstly, practical awareness about the potentials and challenges of co-creation and interaction (participation, accessibility, resources, communication, feasibility, and implementation) more likely will lead to better informed shared decision making in clinical practice, and probably boost the feeling of empowerment on both the patient and provider sides. Secondly, the underlying values that take effect are: the desire to meet at eye level, respecting each other's experiences and values, resource orientation, and vulnerability. I see a true moment of raising the curtain of figure ii and discovering more perspectives from all stakeholders involved, and thus bringing better health outcomes to patients.

If we are able to meet first and foremost as human beings, our expertise will bloom on this ground.

Claudia W., how do you feel about this from your perspective?"

Claudia W.: "I feel really proud that two of our projects led to totally new interventions (RIMA and DITRAS), which were initially developed for research purposes only. By now, they could also be integrated into routine care. In other words, a participatory approach is valuable not only for research but also for implementing changes and innovations in everyday clinical practice. From my experience with the healthcare system, the group at the heart of everything we do—the patients—is often overlooked when discussing process changes or the development of new treatments. That's why for me, the key is emphasizing the importance of raising awareness for the 5P participatory approach in research and clinical practice."

To conclude, what are your thoughts and wishes when you look into the participative future of a tango of five in health care?

Thanks for being with us all the way through this chapter! And enjoy the participation growing as you dance along the following chapters with pharma, payer, and policy.

☆   PROVIDER REFLECTION BOX
      ON PARTICIPATIVE RESEARCH

Earlier, we discussed six areas of governance to make participative research results impactful in daily life. Before we move on, here are some questions to consider with regard to those areas.

- **Participation:** To which stakeholder group would you personally belong to if you would participate in a research project (private, professional, public, or more than one as most people do)? Who could you reach out to in order to learn more about research projects?

- **Accessibility:** What accessibility needs do you have in your everyday life in terms of barrier-free access (i.e. availability to therapy)? How could you contribute to overcome these barriers?

- **Resources:** How much of your time would you be willing to invest in co-creative endeavors in health care? What type of compensation (financial, recognition, co-authorship, vouchers, or other) would best motivate you to participate?

- **Shared language:** Have you ever thought you and your doctor were talking about different things? How can you check in with yourself regularly to recognize and address emotions, to feel more balanced and in control?

- **Implementation:** Have you ever read a scientific study report and thought, "Now, what do I do with this? What does it mean?" What are your ideas to work better together toward feasibility and implementation of results from research to care?

- **Communication:** Where do you most likely inform yourself about innovation and novel research projects? How should scientific research project results be written and visualized to serve as a useful source for you and all stakeholders involved?

CHAPTER 3

The *Pharma* view and the power of public-private partnerships

By Nienke Feenstra

*"Great things are not done by impulse, but by
a series of small things brought together."*

~ VINCENT VAN GOGH

Sitting on the edge of a hospital bed, a twenty-six-year-old man shared how the few minutes of extra time with his family, after having gone through the terrible side effects of chemotherapy due to his osteosarcoma, were worth it. The next day, the man sighed, *"Yes, it is good that the depth of my depression is gone, yet I am so frustrated I cannot have sexual relations with my wife."*

I was interviewing patients in the context of a project on how medication impacts patients' lives. Back then, as a nineteen-year-old pharmacy student, I could not have wished for a more impactful way to learn that the overall value of medication can only be assessed by including the patient's voice.

That was 1992. And, while a lot has changed since then, that profound realization has stayed with me. But as the saying goes, it is easier said than done.

DANCING A COMPLEX TANGO FOR FIVE

Since the late 1990s, the scientific progress and ability to cure diseases has been remarkable. Antiretroviral therapy (ART) has significantly reduced AIDS-related deaths and improved quality of life for those living with HIV. Research stemming out of partnerships between academia and pharma as early as 2008 had shown that patients who were offered ART and whose T-cell counts exceeded a specific threshold one year after ART initiation were reaching a life expectancy approaching that of the general population.[55] Meanwhile, direct-acting antivirals (DAAs) have revolutionized hepatitis C treatment, leading to cure rates exceeding ninety-five per cent and significantly reducing the incidence of liver cirrhosis and patients' risk to succumb to liver cancer.[56] Furthermore, advances in targeted therapy and immuno-oncology have improved survival rates in various cancers with a dramatic bending of the mortality curve as of the 1990s, shown by Verena in her first book, *TangoForFive*.[1] To make that more tangible, as an example, patients with metastatic melanoma are now living forty-four per cent longer since the innovation of immune checkpoint inhibitors that in general have revolutionized cancer care.[57]

Examples like these illustrate the profound impact and power of public-private partnerships (PPP). Bending mortality curves and curing patients from hepatitis is not occurring in isolation. It requires a tight collaboration between pharmaceutical companies, academic researchers, and patients, and often with consultation and input of payers and policymakers.[1] A tango of five.

Figure 3.1: The long and high-risk endeavor to make a difference in people's lives.

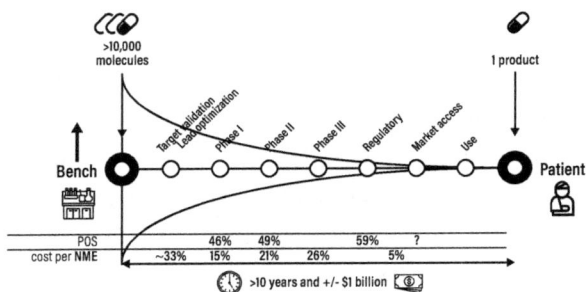

Sources[1, 58]
POS: Probability of Success; NME: New molecule entity.

However, innovation is nothing when it does not reach patients at the end. Drug development is a costly and high-risk endeavor, with only one molecule out of 10,000 from the bench eventually getting to the patient while taking over a decade to deliver.[1, 58]

While everyone agrees that bringing innovation to patients should be a priority, it is not that easy in budget-strained healthcare systems. These systems also face a shortage of health care workers, the need to treat aging populations, and the need to integrate many scientific and digital innovations. All these challenges require investments and financial coverage, meaning we must make tough choices. Choices to ensure that the patient promise of innovation becomes a reality, and that unmet needs are addressed in a sustainable way. Choices that ask the voices of all stakeholders to be heard: the patients, obviously; the increasingly scarce population of health care providers; payers with intense budget challenges to solve; policymakers to ensure innovation at large can become available in an equitable way; and the pharmaceutical and MedTech industry, which develop and manufacture therapeutical innovations.

*It seems obvious to me that solving this dilemma
means dancing a complex tango for five with
everyone sharing risks and responsibility.*

Since my first day in the pharmaceutical industry, I have been passionate about ensuring that innovations can reach patients and that healthcare systems can function in a sustainable way. So, what can the role of a for-profit sector, like the pharmaceutical and MedTech industry or other life sciences, be in this? Asked otherwise: How can the private sector best contribute? Personally, I am convinced that innovation happens faster in a competitive setting and that a for-profit environment helps with setting incentives to deliver. Bending the curve of cancer mortality isn't a coincidence when you consider the booming oncology market in the mid-1990s.[1]

On top of that, in today's healthcare systems, it seems that only pharma has enough of a leverage in their business models to support a full cycle across the seven hurdles of drug development (figure 3.1). It is not only an extremely costly endeavor of over one billion dollars, but moving a product from clinical development to regulatory approval, while ensuring a safe production and distribution at the highest GMP (good manufacturing practice) standards globally, with capabilities to reach all patients in need, usually takes over a decade to accomplish. Despite these hurdles, the prospect of innovation making an impact in people's lives makes me want to be part of this holistic bench-to-bedside cycle each and every day.

But it also comes with responsibility.

_Just like we will only be able to thrive as individuals
on a planet that is sustainable, pharma will only
be able to continue bringing their innovations to
patients in a sustainable healthcare system._

We are working toward a future where innovation supports improving patient health outcomes while reducing environmental impact. We have the responsibility to do what we can, to go above and beyond developing and delivering medicines, and to test, pilot, and scale new strategies while partnering toward (more) sustainable ways of developing, producing, and distributing.

The question thus becomes: What is the best way for the private sector to not only develop and deliver medications, but also to contribute to a more sustainable Value-Based Health Care system that Hanna introduced to us in Chapter 1? Ensuring the right treatment reaches the right patient at the right time?

My aim is to share some of the many real-life examples happening out there and engage you in discovering what is possible.

Are you ready to join me?

Let's go.

WHAT DOES IT TAKE TO MOVE THE NEEDLE?

I echo Verena's sentiment that most people, including those in pharma, work in health care because they are passionate about making a difference to the lives of patients.[1] It almost goes without saying, doesn't it? However, that does not automatically mean the patient's voice is front and center of every decision we are making.

Many good things are done in many companies, like consistently sharing patient testimonials during team meetings, or videos or other content on how patients live with their disease. Sharing the outcomes of patient journey research across an organization, to ensure everyone knows how they directly or indirectly have an impact on patients' lives, is powerful for all hearing this. Whether it concerns a patient advocacy team member who is in direct contact with patients associations, or a finance team member processing an invoice for a patient support tool, having a line of sight of the ultimate impact we have fuels our purpose.

Not everyone knows how patient centricity is expressed in pharmaceutical companies across the entire value chain. Without wanting to be exhaustive or prescriptive, let me share three examples to illustrate that in figure 3.2.

Figure 3.2: Three examples of pharma involvement in bringing patient centricity to life.

Clinical Research	Market Research	Literacy
As you have seen in the chapter 2 on participative research driven by providers, clinical research in general is no more a siloed activity. Active participation with patients is becoming more popular. Similarly, pharma and life sciences involve patients for example when it comes to defining study endpoints.[59] Decentralized technology, health at home concepts in the form of decentralized trial settings enables an even stronger patient involvement as *health happens at home*.[1, 60] Chapter 5 with policymaking is getting into even more detail.	Doing ethnographic market research that shows how patients live with their condition and even adjust their home environment. Like a multiple myeloma patient putting a chair between the door and living room to be able to sit down when needed when opening the door. Only seeing comfortable shoes in the hallway whereas previously high heels were worn.[61] Indicators of change that do not always reach the doctor during consultation and that provide more in-depth understanding of what patients go through.	Pharmaceutical companies develop educational materials for patients to support them in living and understanding their condition. It is a very important tool to contribute to patient empowerment outlined by Hanna in Chapter 1. There is overwhelming data that low health literacy has a detrimental impact on health outcomes.[29, 62] Ensuring that what is made to support patients can add value to them regardless of health literacy level is important.

Remember the quote by Simon Sinek that Hanna and Verena shared in the introduction? *"Happy employees ensure happy customers"* and for us in health care, that is the patient.

Visualizing our patient-centric purpose in a working environment has an impact. It may seem trivial, yet the way we incorporate it, by making it personal, means that employees can have an impact each and every day.

That does not have to be complicated. Asking employees to share how they contribute directly or indirectly to patients' lives, or sharing their wishes for the patients in the future, are very powerful reflections. When the answers are shared visibly in the working environment, it connects people and reinforces purpose.

It is necessary, since wanting to go above and beyond the primary responsibility of a pharmaceutical company—developing a new medication and ensuring it reaches patients—and contributing as well to a more VBHC system is a mammoth task. Later chapters will dive even further into how the intersections in this tango for five make it really hard. Being fueled by purpose helps to stay focused.

For many this is also new. Many outside the pharmaceutical industry do not know how patient centricity is front and center across the value chain in pharma, and how as an industry we aim to contribute to more sustainable healthcare systems. And to be fair, that has not always been the case either. When I started in 1997 in the field of health economics within pharma, I was often asked, *"Is this one of these fashionable new departments that will go away with time?"* or, *"Is it really up to us to look at the impact across society? Isn't that more for governments?"* Luckily it didn't go away. Health economic outcomes research (HEOR) coupled with patient-reported outcomes (PROs) research are now mainstay departments in any company that is in the commercial stage. Of course, exceptions exist. *"There has been abuse of bargaining power and price gouging by a few actors.* [Verena] *is not dwelling on, nor arguing, this point,"* writes Philippe van Holle, former president of Celgene Corporation, in the foreword of *TangoForFive.*[1]

I join Verena in her conclusion, though, that finger pointing and singling out villains won't help anyone fixing healthcare. Generally, my personal observation is that as an industry, we have come a long way to focus and favor value-based approaches that drive patient-centric outcomes. Indeed we are holding ourselves more and more accountable for driving value like never before. I certainly do.

WHICH ENABLERS WILL MAKE
THE TANGO DANCE SMOOTHER?

That being said, let's dive into the main prerequisites and enablers required to move from a detrimental FFS model, which Hanna and Verena outlined so well in the introduction, toward a novel system that puts emphasis on patient outcomes and that rewards activities based on VBHC principles—and the role pharma has to play.

One enabler is digital. Another is novel partnerships. Let's start with the latter.

"Digital is the fuel that ignites the VBHC engine," writes Verena.[1] But digital per se does not have a meaning. What we mean is the electronic capture of relevant patient-centric data.

Figure 3.3: Digital and data are key enablers for pharmaceutical innovation.

There can be no VBHC without data to measure the overall value delivered to patients and the healthcare system, or any specific outcome measures agreed upon for that matter. This is the bread and butter of health care at large. The amount of data that healthcare churns out with each passing second is almost incomprehensible. By 2020, it was estimated that globally the healthcare sector would generate 2.3 zettabytes of data—can you picture that number?? It is 2,300,000,000,000,000,000,000. Or, maybe easier to grasp, the equivalent of 2.3 trillion DVDs worth of movie and video data.[63] Payers, hospitals, and pharma all collect vast quantities of data. And patients are quickly adding to that via applications and wearables.

Given the fact that we collect data continuously, it seems logical to use this data to take steps toward a more VBHC-anchored system.

For this to really take off, we need to ensure the interoperability of different types of health records, the same coding of the data, and policies safeguarding privacy standards of the data.

Data warehouses need to be set up between all stakeholders in health care to ensure everyone contributes and benefits, and we move forward in an aligned way. This cannot be a single stakeholder endeavor as we are working in this tightly interdependent value chain. You will find the payer and policymaker perspectives in later chapters. When it comes to pharma's contribution, I have one recent example fresh in my mind. This is an area where PPPs can really add value, such as the example of AGORiA SANTĒ in France, described here.[64]

AGORiA SANTĒ CONSORTIUM

Launched in June 2021 by the trio partnership of Docaposte, AstraZeneca, and Impact Healthcare, and later joined by Takeda in July 2022, AGORiA SANTĒ aims to facilitate the analysis of real-life health data within a controlled technical and legal framework to improve therapeutic patient care.

With the aim of strengthening the supervision of projects and ensuring appropriate use of health data, the AGORiA SANTĒ consortium is setting up an ethics and scientific committee made up of eleven individuals from the health sector chosen for their expertise and experience in the analysis of health data.

It positions itself as an accelerator for the valorization of health data. Its four members share the conviction that collaboration between different health stakeholders (pharma, laboratories, MedTech, healthcare data producers, hospitals, academic stakeholders, etc.) is at the heart of the acceleration of the digital transformation of health.

In June 2022, the AGORiA SANTĒ consortium was the first consortium of private stakeholders to obtain authorization from the French data privacy authority CNIL to set up a health data warehouse (EDS) with the French national health data system SNDS.

Data warehouses like this are supportive of the move toward VBHC and have the potential to accelerate it. The scale of the initiative asks for both private and public contributions with involvement of policymakers to safeguard privacy and ethical standards, as you will read in more detail in Chapter 5.

Secondly, in a world that is increasingly digital, and a healthcare system that will be transformed by digital in the decade to come, AI and machine learning (ML) will also play a key role for the VBHC transformation. *"Digital makes medicine human again,"* stated Dr Eric Topol, a global leader in scientific and ethical digital transformation in health care.[26]

Pharmaceutical companies are leveraging increasing patient pathway knowledge to develop digital solutions that address pain points in this patient journey. Similarly to what we have learned from our fellow Claudia co-authors, participative research around the patient experience is a cornerstone of value creation. Whether it is to diagnose better, finding and matching doctors and other HCPs faster, or delivering the right intervention to help their symptoms at the right moment, all of these enable patients to share symptoms with their providers to get treatment adaptations as soon as needed, prepare for the visits with their HCPs, get tips on how to integrate the disease management into their daily lives, or use their medication optimally.

Digital solutions are adding value to health care. They improve outcomes, increase care efficiencies, connect various health care providers, and facilitate more remote monitoring.

The startup Elekta Kaiku prides itself on pioneering the personalization of cancer care through the use of apps and wearables collecting data that are important for patients.

A prospective multicenter study involving colorectal cancer patients treated with oxaliplatin-based adjuvant chemotherapy—known to cause severe neuropathy in the majority of patients—revealed an important finding via the startup's remote patient monitoring (RPM) tool.[65] Although the disabling neuropathy can't be completely avoided nor effectively treated, the RPM use of electronic patient-reported outcomes (ePROs) led to an earlier detection of low sensibility or tingling in fingertips and toes, so that dose adjustments could be made earlier and therefore overall leading to less disease burden introduced through side effects from chemotherapy.[66]

This is what we mean when we refer to "outcomes that matter to patients." Living longer or being cured through chemo, but still being able to button shirts and being able to feel fingers well enough to swipe on an iPad. Both daily activities become impossible if you suffer from severe peripheral neuropathy. Not only did this study prove the impact for the individual patient, but it also showed that the RPM-assisted PROMs collection led to a fifty-seven per cent reduction in phone call burden for healthcare systems, while eighty-five per cent of patients felt that Elekta Kaiku improved their overall health status.

The beauty of many digital solutions is that they automatically allow us to collect and transmit data in real-time, tailored to a need, and hence creating value. For patients. For the system. It is not only a great tool for enhanced provider-patient relationships, as demonstrated in Chapter 2, but it also opens the door to create value-based agreements with payers (more on that in Chapter 4).

We call it *whole value* when such a combination of a therapeutic medicine coupled with a digital tool is delivered as a one-stop-shop innovation to patients and healthcare systems alike.

So, why not take steps to ensure this overall value will be recognized by healthcare systems? More on that later.

THE NEXT STEP IS FOSTERING PARTNERSHIPS ANCHORED IN TRUST

"We are facing a crisis of trust," elaborates Philippe von Holle, *"or mistrust between the five actors and between pharma and society."*[1] Forging novel partnerships to deliver whole value can't be achieved in silos. It requires trust among all required stakeholders in health care. Patients will only use solutions that will really help them live with their disease better if they know their data is being treated correctly. HCPs will only use solutions that are integrated with their clinic systems, delivering data they trust to base their care interventions on. Payers will only pay for outcomes when they trust the data delivered to them via claims datasets. All this requires good policy frameworks and solution-focused co-creation, enabling the necessary trust. Trust can also be built by innovation incrementally. Knowing a first small step works well, will it be possible to take a larger, second step?

Various stakeholders in health care have expressed doubt on whether pharma should be at the start of such partnership initiatives at all, stating that being for-profit would somehow render them less credible. Really—why? With the right framework, the right policies (i.e. on data privacy and data protection), and a solid ethical committee approval process, I'm saying that this kind of partnership research and development is feasible and can benefit patients. I think we would be amiss to put them—and the knowledge pharmaceutical companies have on the therapeutic areas they operate in, and develop medical and additional solutions for—aside.

Indeed, paying for health instead of having fees for service is a huge step, a true transformation.

In established healthcare systems, this transformation will not be feasible overnight. Too much legacy built in stone—i.e. large hospital systems and deeply anchored multipage policy frameworks—needs to be reformed. Hence a need for small steps that can contribute to building trust while leveraging (digital) data.

For countries with large-scale national reimbursement systems, a full-risk reform to pay for the value of an entire cycle of care can be too big of a step (for details, refer to Chapters 4 and 5). In that case, going small-scale local, i.e. one hospital at a time, might be a more viable first step.

Let me illustrate how pharma can be a proactive partner in this with a practical example.

Imagine a scenario with a company having developed a combination of a product, plus a service app allowing patients living with a chronic disease, such as diabetes, to do these three things:

- reporting symptoms remotely to enable earlier interventions and better outcomes (i.e. avoiding unnecessary visits);
- requesting the next delivery of their product precisely only once on a specific day (i.e. avoiding drug wastage); and
- asking questions of their doctors and nurses when needed to adjust and find optimal dosing (i.e. saving precious health care worker time).

Now, we could imagine several options on how to bring this product to market—more or less effectively; more or less collaboratively; more or less value-generating. One option could be: hospitals buying the drug and the app separately, each with a price tag—the old way. We could also imagine the combined offering being part of a hospital tender for a fixed price—gaining one additional level of synergy and cost savings. A third option could be a fixed fee for that combination with additional incentive payments based on the outcomes achieved through the drug-app combo, reaping patient-powered efficiencies. And a last option would be to fully and only base payments on predefined patient outcome improvements—a full-risk, value-based model.

See the pattern? Siloed product deployment may introduce areas of waste because although both drug and app mutually would enhance their effects, the use and payments would remain decoupled from the impact on the patient. These four different options could also be viewed as an incremental step-by-step implementation process over a certain period of time to allow the parties to adapt an outcome measurement data infrastructure and the respective financial and legal payment frameworks.

It is just one of many examples to illustrate how small steps can be meaningful to build trust, learn how to leverage data in a partnership approach, and, through that, take steps toward more *value-based* health care that puts outcomes that matter to patients first.

FROM LOCAL PILOTS TO GLOBAL IMPACT

Writing about theory is fine. But checking in on real-life progress is what really matters. What has already been done in local partnership work involving different stakeholders to pilot and learn? A couple of these are showcased in figure 3.4.

Figure 3.4: Examples of local partnerships, powered by AI and digital.

Expediting patient access	Beyond the pill
For patients with hereditary angioedema a new prophylactic drug was brought to market with a simple outcome-based agreement with the local Ministry of Health, based on volume of injections. In case patients needed more than a certain predefined amount as a proxy for effectiveness the company took the financial risk and paid for it. Qualification of patients for that treatment was supported by an application developed by the company that allowed patients to have their photo taken during an attack. That photo would be sent to the treating physician and could be uploaded into the patient file. Small steps that brought the doctor, the payer and the patient together around usage of data, creating trust to build on for the future.[61]	Pharmaceutical companies partner with Startups in the field of (ultra-)rare diseases to analyze hospital records in different departments. Patients with rare conditions often visit different specialists, all holding a piece of the diagnostic puzzle, without being able to combine these pieces. AI enables to combine these insights across records. This faster diagnosis lowers numbers of unnecessary doctors' visits and tests, brings the right treatment as soon as possible, and thus promises better clinical outcomes for patients. A clear example of optimization of resources. Offering this AI device in combination with a therapy is a holistic approach. It brings start-up, pharma, hospitals and patients closer together. Including payers into these collaborations is a logical consequence. [67]

The motto is thus "think big and start small." Small steps that allow us to learn and create trust, that can and will serve as a platform for bolder action. If it is not possible to have a project with all five actors all the time, start with two or three. If it is not possible to do something nationally, go regionally or hospital-by-hospital. The main thing is to get going and make a start. Breaking a challenge down into smaller steps will always bring a solution forward. A true marathon of baby steps to increase patient value.

Small steps alone will not be enough, though, to truly transform entire healthcare systems. We also need big-ticket items to challenge the healthcare status quo. Larger-scale PPPs like the World Economic Forum's Global Coalition for Value in Healthcare, and the Innovative Health Initiative (IHI) project H2O.

The World Economic Forum, with leading industry and academic partners, has made big strides to move the needle on VBHC transformation over the past decade through the Global Coalition for Value in Healthcare.[68, 69] Its focus is multifold as depicted in figure 3.5. In brief, and as nicely animated in a TEDx-style conversation by Hanna with Yasmin Dias-Guichot at the 5P Flagship Event 2023, it covers data, partnerships, and payments in a crisp way.[70]

One of the primary goals is to develop and implement standardized outcome measures that can be used globally. This ensures that health care providers and payers can compare outcomes across different regions and healthcare systems. The coalition advocates for the creation of interoperable data systems that allow for the seamless exchange of healthcare data. This is crucial for measuring outcomes and ensuring that patients receive the best possible care.

It further works to promote the adoption of value-based payment models that reward HCPs for delivering high-quality care rather than the volume of services provided. And lastly, by bringing together diverse stakeholders, the coalition fosters collaboration and encourages the sharing of best practices. This helps to accelerate the adoption of VBHC practices globally.

Figure 3.5: The cross of VBHC partnerships—adaptation from source.[69]

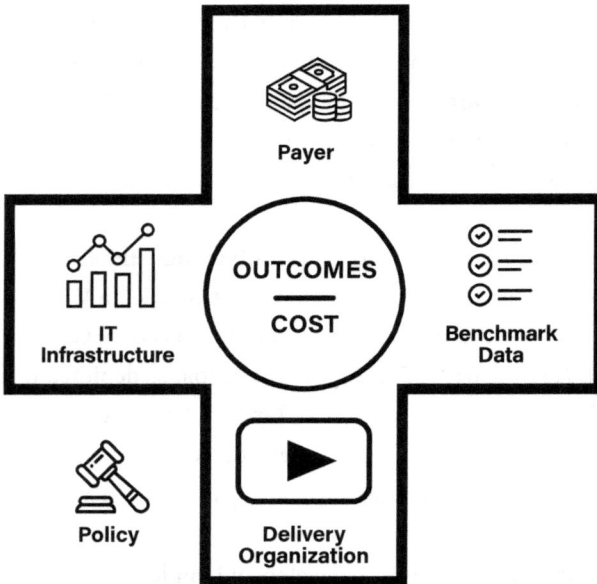

Another one of these big-ticket items, as I call them, is the Health Outcomes Observatory (H2O).[71] An Innovative Health Initiative on the European level, it focuses on diabetes, inflammatory bowel disease (IBD), and oncology. H2O established standardized outcomes metrics through multistakeholder consensus using standard sets of PROMs.[72]

The emphasis of the project is to create a common language between patients and physicians to empower patients to monitor their outcomes digitally and enable shared decision making. These standardized interactions between patients and physicians generate data that are being aggregated and managed by independent legal entities that function as data trusts, with boards representing all stakeholders. The data governance model has been set up in each participating country with an independent multistakeholder board, including providers, payers, policymakers, and patient advocacy groups—partnerships that foster trust in the network. This collaboration ensures that the project addresses the needs and concerns of *all* stakeholders, and promotes the adoption of VBHC practices such as transparency of patient outcomes. It allows for the aggregation and analysis of health data from different countries, providing valuable insights into healthcare outcomes and best practices. As a result of the initiative, at the time of writing this, there are now health outcome observatories operating as data trusts in the Netherlands, Austria, Germany, and Spain, with a pan-European umbrella organization based in Denmark.

The standardized use of clinical outcomes and PROMs ensures that HCPs and payers can consistently measure and compare patient outcome data across different regions and healthcare systems. This allows both patients and physicians to understand how each patient compares to a cohort of patients with similar conditions and needs across Europe, and therefore facilitates shared decision making. The consortium emphasizes patient autonomy over their own health data, anchored in the H2O patient agreement. This does not only foster the well-described need for patient empowerment from Chapter 1, but it also ensures that the actual data collected are relevant and meaningful. H2O has established a data access model, securing the possibility to use the health data for any 'bona fide' research query.

I am deeply convinced that this combination of global big-ticket items and local practice steps will leave no stone unturned and no step without impact for patients.

CONCLUDING THE TANGO OF
PUBLIC-PRIVATE PARTNERSHIPS

With the enablers being clear, and local and global initiatives starting to move the needle, I am asking: What does it take to advance collaborative value-based principles for all actors from a pharma perspective?

Along the value chain, I see *patients* wanting and needing to take control of their own health, and their data. A starting point for me is the continuous dialogue on where the real pain points in the patient journey are. I wish for continued *provider* openness to co-create, leading to a foundation of trust to support transparency of outcomes data. It requires breaking down barriers of data interoperability, workflows, and culture on all sides of the tango fence. Learning about the cited pain points in the patient journey requires the co-design of the best possible care pathways. As alluded to, I encourage *payers* within multiyear partnerships anchored in a willingness to look beyond the budget silo. Horizon scannings will be crucial tools to make this sustainable, and to move toward payment based on overall value delivered. That can go step-by-step by including additional value provided by, among others, *pharma* companies that have a positive impact on care pathways, and clinical and well-being outcomes in value assessments. Lastly, we all need a strategic and proactive relationship with *policymakers* to ensure privacy and ethical frameworks are in place, allowing for research and swift uptake of breakthrough innovations.

My last call for action is a call on leadership.

Unwavering leadership demonstrating courage and collaboration, fueled by passion to make a difference in patients' lives together. No wonder Verena placed it in her top ten for health care transformation in *TangoForFive*.[1] I feel strongly that each and every leader across the 5P value chain will need to translate patient needs and their contribution to a sustainable healthcare system into a compelling vision for their organization, ensuring that the capabilities required to reach that vision are present.

The journey toward VBHC is a complex and challenging one, but it is also a journey that holds immense promise for improving patient outcomes and creating more sustainable healthcare systems. By focusing on data, digital solutions, partnership and trust, innovative contracting across budget years and silos, and leadership, organizations can make meaningful progress toward this goal.

The combination of leadership in global big-ticket items such as the Global Coalition for Value in Healthcare and the H2O

Observatory, along with local practical steps forward, will have a significant impact.

Achieving this vision requires unwavering leadership,
a patient-centered organizational structure, and
a fundamental shift in mindset and capabilities.

That will not be easy since there will be many obstacles and subsequent learnings along the way. At these moments, when the challenge seems too intense, when people might say, "This will never happen," I mentally go back to those moments interviewing patients in 1992. I think of the impact we can have on patients' lives today and tomorrow, in a sustainable healthcare system, and keep going with the other 5Ps to identify the next step.

I invite you to reflect on the following topics, which will help you to foster that fundamental mindset shift and the development of new capabilities within organizations in the private sector. As Vincent van Gogh said, *"Great things are not done by impulse, but by a series of small things brought together."*

PHARMA REFLECTION BOX ON
PUBLIC-PRIVATE PARTNERSHIPS

The tango of public-private partnerships was a key focus in this chapter. Before we move on, here are some questions to consider in relation to this.

- **Value-based, patient-first mindset:** Can you focus on delivering high-quality care—improving patient outcomes rather than increasing the volume of services and medicines only—i.e. rethinking traditional business models?

- **Data-driven decision making:** Can you help foster the capability to collect, analyze, and use data to drive shared decision making? How can you invest in data infrastructure, including data analytics capabilities, to promote a culture of data-driven decision making?

- **Trust and partnership:** What is your role to achieve VBHC in partnership with others—providers, payers, policymakers, and patient advocacy groups? How can you build and maintain these partnerships, fostering trust as you work toward common goals?

- **Digital innovation and iteration:** What culture of innovation can you nurture? How can you remain open to new ideas, reaping the full benefits and impact of digital innovations?

- **Think big and start small:** What is your first step toward VBHC? Take one stakeholder at a time. Provide opportunities to learn. Take bigger steps next time. Never stop working to foster trust.

CHAPTER 4

The *Payer* view on sharing risk and co-creating value

By Caitlin Masters and Verena Voelter

"We need a way to pay for health care that
fosters the delivery of superior value to patients."

~ MICHAEL PORTER

One of the peculiarities of health care is that the buyer doesn't directly interact with the seller.

What do we mean? As you have noticed in the preceding chapters, no doctor-patient relationship, no health care. But the provider isn't the one who is selling, and the patient isn't buying from the provider either (at least in parts). Doctors are technically selling their services, such as consults and surgeries, but they are not selling the much-needed treatments, such as prescription pills or cancer immuno-chemotherapies. These are developed and provided by what we read from Nienke Feenstra in Chapter 3—the pharma sector, or at large the private MedTech and life sciences sectors.

So, who pays?

Well, in health care, as much as all of the actors in the 5P value chain weigh into the cost part of the value equation, who actually carries the most power to decide what is or isn't reimbursed and paid for? Who decides on the value and a price tag for a pill or a procedure? The answer is: the *payers*. That is one of the many peculiarities in health care because this independent body—such as a health insurance or a health plan—is actually paying the bills for what a doctor and a patient agree to do. Yes, that's a trio, and not a group of five (which would include pharma and policymakers), and this set of three is complex and interdependent enough on its own. What makes it even more complex is that certain countries work with central payer systems (i.e. France, Spain, Israel) where the payer and the policymaker share health authority function, whereas others decentralize their health plan ownerships into the regions (i.e. the various States in the US, the Bundesländer in Germany, and the Cantons in Switzerland). For the purpose and sake of this book, we won't dwell too much on those payer intricacies. Rather, we'll assume that one body in each country has to pay the bill.

This is who we refer to as the *payer*.

Generally speaking, what payers need most is certainty about the forecast. Knowing that the planned spending for their covered population will not be surpassed by the end of the year, hence budget control is front and center in their interests. Usually, healthcare budgets are somehow linked and controlled by a policy body such as governments and health ministries. Within an allocated envelope of budget, payers can set the rate, couple reimbursement with quality measures in their contracts with providers and pharma, and make team-based, patient-centric care the standard. Now, in practice, this is challenging because multiple interests from at least three of the 5Ps in the payment chain (payer, provider, pharma) need to be aligned, but it is the payers who are pushing forward toward novel payment models, as they have learned that it is a good way to ascertain budget allocations meeting demand.

This chapter is meant to inform you of the key ingredients in this recipe, showcasing what payers can do to align financial incentives and to make patient centricity real.

WHO IS THE MAIN ACTOR?

To start, let me (Caitlin) go back a couple of years in my own life and share with you a personal story of how payers can impact the first days of a child's life and of a woman's journey into motherhood. I am a senior expert in value-based partnerships in my work life, and a proud young mom in my private life.

Let me share with you this compelling story of my first child being born.[73]

Only four days after giving birth to my first girl, I felt exhausted and woke up with a fever. Of course, I had no experience with this—it was my first baby! "Do I need to go to the ER? What do hours of waiting in the ER do to the baby? All the bugs and germs—and COVID-19?' All of these thoughts were spinning in my head.

Let me provide you with a couple of technical details around how I eventually returned home with a happy baby and all the care I needed.

My *kraamverzorgster* (maternity nurse) had taken my temperature as part of the daily check. Within minutes, she contacted my midwife who then contacted the doctor in the clinic. Note number one: both had looked after me during my childbirth. An hour later, I was back at the same ward, on the same floor, with the same team that knew about my situation. Note number two: all with my husband and baby safely at my side, and no ER! Within the hour that followed, I had gotten the right blood draws and right urine tests, confirming that I had a rare combination of two infections at the same time: mastitis and cystitis. A serious situation if not diagnosed and treated promptly. Note number three: luckily for me, being in the Netherlands, I had started my treatment for the right diagnosis at the right time! No unnecessary exams done.

As part of the Dutch insurance scheme, the *Kraamzorg* is a post-natal care service provided to a new mother and her baby, with a maternity nurse coming to the mom's home for the first seven days postpartum. This nurse plays a central role in better health outcomes of moms and babies, and is at the bonding core of the care continuum for a new mother—rather than traditional siloed care in an OBGYN department on the one hand, and a pediatric department on the other. *"Health and health care start and end at home,"* as Verena wrote in *TangoForFive*.[1] How lucky I was to live in a country following this practice!

For me, it meant no unnecessary stay in an overloaded ER, which would pose two additional problems: an increased risk of catching yet another infection in crowded corridors; and seeing providers who had no idea of my situation, nor were specialized in OBGYN matters. This would—you can guess it—increase unnecessary cost.

The learnings?

It showcases beautifully the essentials of patient centricity.

———————

Through optimal provider-payer alignment powered by digitally enabled solutions such as wearables and telehealth apps, it focuses on what truly matters to patients in a pathway that is designed for what patients really need along their health journey.

———————

This Dutch example of a standardized *Kraamzorg* system is enabled by a tight alignment between provider, payers, and policymakers within a legal framework, a compliant flow of data, and payments to all actors for what the patient actually needs—across all critical intersections, including the hospital-at-home gap. I will get back to this example later on when we showcase novel payment models.

THE NEED TO ALIGN AN ENTIRE CYCLE OF CARE

In the US, I've been working across the 5Ps of the healthcare industry since the 2010s. Most of my experience is in forging provider-payer partnerships. The first time I saw a true value-based care (VBC) program was when I was working for a payer and saw the creation of a total medical expense program. By looking at the highest-risk, highest-cost patients with physical and mental health co-morbidities, a cohort of about 10,000 patients was identified, and the payer and select providers worked together with payer and provider staff to contact and enroll these patients in the program. Five years later, I moved to the provider side and ran a VBC program at a physician group connected to an academic medical center where the variety of pay-for-performance contracts and value-based programs we enrolled made it difficult to align incentives, physicians, and patient needs (and wants!).

To be successful, my team and I worked with payers to forge deep partnerships with the ones most interested in collaborating.

We worked together by sharing data back and forth, understanding which patients they see as high-risk versus what our data told us, and teaching one another our methods and practices to care for and manage patients.

As COVID-19 hit, things rapidly changed in my personal life and I made the jump across the ocean to Amsterdam. In some ways it felt like starting over, but, in others, it created a whole new world for me as I networked with key additional VBC players, one of them being Verena. Shortly after we met, we began collaborating and co-writing articles, unlocking the future of health care through the 5Ps. Truth be told, the actors along the 5P value chain jointly create the foundation to effective patient-centric, value-based care by forging novel partnerships. Verena and I are acutely aware that each 'P' has their own interests and priorities, so working together means negotiating (more on this by Suzanne in Chapter 6!).

In their bestselling business strategy book, *The Ends Game: How Smart Companies Stop Selling Products and Start Delivering Value,*

Marco Bertini and Oded Koenigsberg ask, *"Would you rather pay for healthcare or for better health?"*[74] Of course, the only thing we all want is better and sustained health for us and our beloved ones.

Figure 4.1: The HHH transition: the hospital-to-home intersection often is a hurdle where information gets lost in space and time.

HHH
Hospital-Home Hurdle

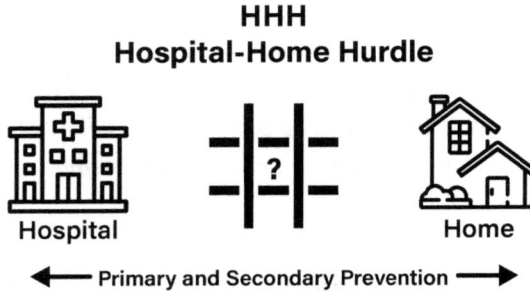

Hospital   ?   Home

← **Primary and Secondary Prevention** →

Caitlin's story shows that bridging and aligning the financial incentives across the 5Ps within an entire cycle of care leads to breaking down of silos that are at the root cause of driving low-value care. In her personal hospital-to-home transition, each care team member involved in her giving-birth medical condition received reimbursement for following their specific role and responsibility, communicating across the care coordination team (as alluded to by Hanna in Chapter 1), and following standard escalation protocols when something was amiss. Not only that, but the financial incentive structure also allowed for the hospital-at-home (H@H) concept to be the standard of care, driving patient centricity.

When we look at the VBHC equation—outcomes that matter to patients divided by its costs— it seems we are achieving true value.

Outside of this example, though, health care for most of us is not this seamless because the financial incentives across the 5Ps are not aligned with the outcomes that matter to patients. Despite the astronomical amount of money spent on health care delivery, each of the 5Ps still works in a silo, which is fueling the high-cost spiral.[1] As alluded to in the preface, healthcare expenditure is rising without an end in sight (figure i) while 5P actors blame each other mutually for who the supposed villain is. Since *TangoForFive* was published in 2021, we have updated the main categories of spending and the picture remains grim, with waste remaining a centerpiece for the broken balance between innovation and affordability (figure 4.2).[75-83]

Figure 4.2: Leading causes of healthcare expenditure in three different countries.

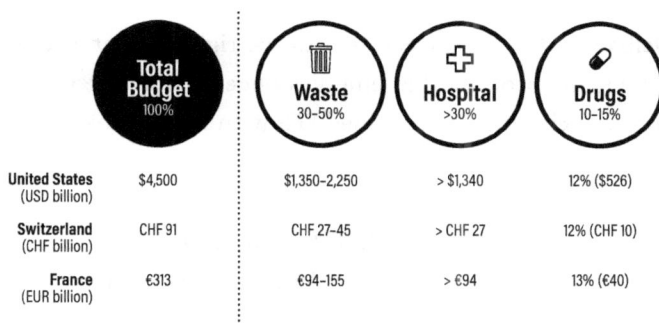

	Total Budget 100%		Waste 30–50%	Hospital >30%	Drugs 10–15%
United States (USD billion)	$4,500		$1,350–2,250	> $1,340	12% ($526)
Switzerland (CHF billion)	CHF 91		CHF 27–45	> CHF 27	12% (CHF 10)
France (EUR billion)	€313		€94–155	> €94	13% (€40)

Sources[75-83]

The ongoing issue being that the current FFS system—which disconnects payments from patient benefit—is built in silos and hospitals structured to service administrative flows and not the patient journey, so that it is impossible to measure the cost along an entire patient journey, or "cycle of care" as the healthcare payment pathway is usually referred to. Michael Porter put it simply years ago when he said, *"The fee-for-service system is now perhaps the single biggest obstacle to improving health care delivery."*[84]

The silos are built in a way that you can depict from Caitlin's experience. They leave big gaps along the hurdles between patient-provider-pharma-payer-policy if not bridged by measures to manage those intersections effectively along the patient journey, such as novel roles like a *kraamverzorgster*, and interoperable digital data capture.

Moving the needle from selling volume and quantity of services toward outcomes that matter and quality of care delivered along a full cycle of care is what will bring true value for all actors.

Delivering the right treatment to the right patient at the right time is the promise that emerges once we start breaking silos and replacing an old-fashioned FFS with future-looking VBHC.

OUTCOMES THAT MATTER TO PATIENTS—MEASURE QUALITY

Most of the time, quality isn't actually looked at—or often enough only as an afterthought or check-box exercise requested by some unknown administrators. Sound familiar? Hanna already called it out as a big warning sign.

In a system that incentivizes doing *more* of the same, the attention to how *well* our actions impact the patient's health isn't part of the game. How do we usually rank restaurants, holiday experiences, or an Uber ride? Right, with our five-star ranking system within a thirty-second swipe on our smartphone. That's what we mean by delivering outcomes that matter to our customers.

In health care? It's not yet an institutionalized—or cultivated—behavior.

In places where the focus is shifting, and emphasis put on both patient and health care worker satisfaction—along the lines of VBHC's formula of putting the cost in relation to the outcomes delivered—we do see glimpses of hope on the horizon. In the US, the National Quality Measures Clearinghouse (NQMC), under the hospices of the Department of Health and Human Services (HHS), helps providers and payers with an accessible mechanism for obtaining detailed information on quality measures. It promotes an environment for further dissemination of quality-related measures, and their implementation, in order to inform better health care decision making.[85, 86] In many places, the issue being that still the vast majority of data and measures collected are actually *not* related to patients. A landmark article on measuring outcomes, by VBHC experts Dr Thomas Lee and Dr Michael Porter in 2016, illustrated the extent of the dilemma with so-called QIs collecting *provider-process*-related measures more than two-thirds of the time, while only one-third of all QIs were actually gathering *patient-related* outcome measures.[87]

Putting it differently, it's a FFS system turned to absurdity, forcing providers to deliver more processes rather than incentivizing results that are relevant to the real customer—the patient.

A new way of fostering high-quality care delivery while maintaining customer centricity is to map and coordinate all actors and activities that are required to achieve a desired outcome.

Translating the incentive structure within a full cycle of care into a pathway that can generate more efficient payment structures is the additional true value of starting with the end in mind: results that matter to patients. As outlined in great detail by Hanna in Chapter 1, the three-step VBHC process (figure 1.6) is catering to this objective as we apply it within our day job consulting work: defining a population of patients with similar needs, mapping all clinical and non-clinical actors required, to finally obtain desired outcomes.[5]

Once we are aware of what those activities are, we can start measuring an entire cycle of care. For example, in the Dutch Diabeter 5P consortium, patients and families of children with T1D are rallying behind the defined outcomes for a given annual year (i.e. reducing ER visits or HbA1c levels) and whoever is needed to achieve that goal from the proverbial round table (not only patients, nurses, and doctors, but also schools, sport clubs, and nutritionists) is collectively entering the data they need to measure procedures, medicines, and other interventions to achieve this outcome.[1, 88]

MAKING THE VALUE EQUATION
THE STANDARD OF CARE

Patient centricity means collecting and measuring data that truly matter to patients, as you've read about in the H2O example in Chapter 3. However, in systems originally built on pen, paper, and fax machines, scaling relevant health data for benchmarking and data mining—to determine the best quality care for an entire population—is challenging. Therefore, it is also hard to spin the full circle of an entire patient journey.

*However, you can't improve nor manage
what you can't measure.*

In legacy FFS systems, payers hold a wealth of data. Also, because they can see the full continuum of claims submitted for a patient, they hold quite a bit of power. Fundamental to VBHC is a standardized data capture framework to ensure automatic data transfer between payers and providers. Both of them need to see the full picture of the patient: the provider needs to understand where the patient has been outside their own four walls; and the payer needs to be aware of the patient experience via PROMs and PREMs. For example, for care at home models, such as H@H, to become the standard of care, standardized data capture and transfer will be critical to prove their success. Standardization will allow us to compare and benchmark longitudinally whether the delivery of care in these H@H models is the same or better than the standard of care model.

In the *Kraamzorg* story, the patient—Caitlin—was at the center of care and data exchange. It enabled the seamless communication between the relevant stakeholders of the proverbial round table and helped all actors, including payers, accessing claims data. Improving outcomes. Reducing cost. Fueled by data exchange in connectivity driven by digital technology.

To help us further grasp the idea of what a perfect patient-provider-payer partnership could look like, we'd like to recap a recent anecdote of Verena's nephew that nearly ended in a fatal drama.

Let's call him Jim.

PREVENTING HEART FAILURE?

Picture a healthy, forty-year-old man in the most perfect shape of his life.

A policeman in the ranks of team responsibility, his physical shape had been exemplary for many years and he had a good work-life balance. Then, one day on duty before lunch, he felt recurring heartburn. A quick check at the GP a few days earlier hadn't given any hints, with ECG being normal. His girlfriend continued to pressure him to go and consult a specialist, observing his increasing troubles with pain unrelated to any sports, eating, or physical efforts.

He gave in and called the cardiologist one calm morning on the job. The doctor offered him a free slot right after lunch the same day, or an appointment next month. Thankfully, he made the right choice to consult the doctor straightaway.

Similar scenario as at the GP's: heart echography and ECG didn't show much. But after checking some family history with Jim, it was revealed that Jim's dad had multiple heart attacks, the first one at age forty-five. Bingo, a family predisposition. The cardiologist reacted immediately and put Jim on a spinning cycle to perform a cardio stress test. Bingo again! While under stress, Jim started developing a massive myocardial infarction.

Fast forward to an hour later, an interventional cardiologist was joking with a pain-free Jim in the catheter lab while being in awe at what was a total block of the main anterior coronary artery. Swiftly implanting a stent, the heart muscle instantly revitalized.

Had a total blocking and heart attack occurred during Jim's scuba dive the weekend before, he would have died. At the age of forty, leaving behind an orphaned son, aged ten.

In the HHH transition between hospital and home (figure 4.1), would Jim's episode have been preventable?

Likely, yes. For two reasons.

Firstly, a family history of early-onset heart attacks should have prompted careful and close observations and lifestyle measures to delay and prevent a full coronary artery block in the first place. Secondly, a tailored care plan made to accommodate his choices in life—being an active policeman on duty and regularly doing high-intensity workouts—could have been applied and protected his health without compromising the kind of life he loves.

THE STEP TO PERSONALIZED
HEALTH CARE IS RISK STRATIFICATION

One-size-fits-all care is like the good being the enemy of the great. We've heard it from Hanna.

In Jim's case, prevention and precaution would have been the essential first step to avoid his heart attack, or at least substantially decrease the risk of dying from it. Given his positive family history, regular checks using ECG, stress tests and echocardiography would have been indicated according to the guidelines of acute myocardial infarction (AMI) and acute coronary syndrome (ACS), coupled with adequate fat lowering and cardio-protective medication and dietary restrictions.[89-91]

However, if we read these guidelines for "a general case" of positive AMI family history, plus hypercholesteremia, the generic recommendations read: in addition to specific medication, keep a low-fat diet, exercise moderately, and maintain a healthy weight.[92]

Would that have been ideal for Jim?

Likely no.

Because where would the six hours of CrossFit per week fit in? The regular scuba dives? And the active policy duty wearing a full gear of ten kilograms?

*One-size-fits-all is not leading to improved
outcomes for an entire population living
with the same medical condition.*

Preparing patients for the HHH transition (figure 4.1) with a leaf-let at discharge, and clear instructions on how to go about their lives as they go home, is a very good measure. For an individual patient, it's a very good first step toward what Hanna alluded to earlier: patient empowerment, care coordination, and a holistic view to illness "beyond the pill."

But it is also a very bad measure when you look at it from a pop-ulation-health perspective.

Why?

I (Verena) would venture to say that Jim would not have adhered to these generic guidelines as they did not match his lifestyle and sporty needs. Luckily for Jim, he had taken different actions.

"Verena, I applied what you wrote in your first book! I did 'patient empowerment'!" he reported proudly. Curious what he was refer-ring to specifically, I learned that he proactively inquired to be seen by a specialist HCP called a sports cardiologist.[93] There, he found what he needed. A personalized care plan that looks more similar to a coaching plan from a high-end fitness club than a specialty medicine plan. He had co-created with his new doctor a detailed hourly and weekly workout agenda, coupled with dietary and nutrition choices fitting his need for high-calorie and protein-rich

nutrition (even building in self-care moments for the occasional glass of whiskey!).

It is living in practice what Hanna introduced to us in Chapter 1: caring for the six dimensions in the Wheel of Health (figure 1.4). Balance all your needs to obtain optimal results for your own health.

From a VBHC process perspective, we refer to this tailoring of plans as population risk stratification.

Within two to four risk strata, simple groupings of patients share the same medical condition as per the World Health Organization (WHO) categories of the International Classification of Diseases (ICD-10) code. They come with a very different set of personal needs and choices depending on: the number and kind of co-morbidities; smoker or not; overweight or not; including lifestyle choices and work-related situations (i.e. employed, retired, student). One very simple, yet highly effective way to cluster a population into four simple strata is applied by the team at Oak Street Health (OSH) as cited in *TangoForFive*.[1] In brief, well, average, sick, and very sick risk groups allow OSH to tailor home care needs and doctor visit schedules to various degrees. This simple measure reduced (unnecessary) hospital admission rates by a staggering forty-one per cent.

In the case of Jim and his 'peer group' population of AMI (ICD-10 code I21), a simple set of three strata may reap massive impact from a population-health perspective—see our suggestions for a "3S of AMI" stratification in figure 4.3.

Figure 4.3: Example of risk stratification: the "3S of AMI" (acute myocardial infarction) ICD-10 code I21.

RISK STRATA	POPULATION	CRITERIA
1. STRONG	• No co-morbidities • Independent living • High degree of health and digital literacy • High degree of self-motivation & empowerment	• Limited follow-up, in-person doctor visits, more telehealth • Use of Apps & wearables to self-monitor/report symptoms • Consult specialty care (ie sports medicine, nutrition) • Coaching support for wheel of health measures
2. SUPPORT	• 2 to 3 co-morbidities (ie metabolic condition) • Light degree of cognitive dysfunctioning • Reduced mobility, but independent living • Special needs in ≥2 dimensions of the wheel of health	• Tailored follow-up in-person GP visits coordinating specialty appointments, including mental health if needed • Use of Apps to support symptom monitoring and PROMS – consider investing in wearables – select telehealth • Coaching for select wheel of health measures
3. SICK	• Karnowski index <50 - Very limited mobility • Multiple co-morbidities • Living support needed, including medication dispense • ≥2 hospital stays per year	• H@H opportunities • Caregiver resources tailored to support special needs and co-morbidities; socioeconomic family support • Complementary telehealth for specialty care

MAKING IT HAPPEN

How does this all relate to the payer's perspective? Does it address the need and interest for cost containment, in-budget planning, and certainty of money spent on the right patients in need?

Yes, it does.

There are two main components to make patient centricity work for VBHC: one is generally referred to as *time-dependent activity-based costing* (TD-ABC), and the other revolves around mutual agreements on *value-based contracting*. The former is lining up all activities in the middle "triangle" section of figure 1.6 in Chapter 1, and mapping cost to each of these activities required to obtain the desired outcome. For the interested reader, we refer to an ample base of literature as well as the work of the TDABC in Healthcare Consortium under the leadership of Dr Ana Etges.[94-95] The latter is taking the risk stratification, such as that used by OSH or the suggestive one for AMI in figure 4.3, and thus enabling all actors of the 5P value chain to co-create best possible options and agreements to meet a common goal.

Specifically, the payer always has to satisfy a triad of measures: the number of required consults (i.e. costly and time-consuming in-person or efficient telehealth visits); amount of prescription drugs and interventions (i.e. statins, coronarography, or bypass surgeries); and c) investments chosen into prevention and education programs. Remember, an eighty-five-year old with AMI may have very different needs and goals in life than a forty-year old sports enthusiast preparing for the next marathon.

In order to illustrate novel payment models and possible value-based agreements, we are showcasing a number of examples, grouped into two axes of collaboration within the 5P value chain:

1. Caitlin is sharing personal experiences from various payer-*provider* models for outcomes-based care delivery; and

2. Verena shares an example of payer-*pharma* contracting for risk-sharing of innovative medicines and interventions.

1. Novel payment models in care delivery

For a payer to become patient-centric, the move away from traditional FFS means adopting new payment models that require a change in engagement and collaboration with providers. The myriad of models can be laid along a continuum, allowing for higher reward and risk as engagement and collaboration between payers and providers matures (see figure 4.4).

Figure 4.4: Options for payer-provider contracting models. The models become increasingly patient-centric as the foundational elements—risk, quality, shared savings—deepen and as providers and payers engage and collaborate more intensively with one another.

		Risk Stratification	Quality reporting linked to incentives	Shared Savings
Models require increasing engagement and collaboration between payers & providers	**Capitation**	At the population level (Most often includes upside risk only)	Often time includes process and outcome measures	Generally, not
	Bundled Payments	Limited scope to episode and condition (Upside and downside risk possible; most models start with upside risk only)	Limited scope to episode and condition	Limited scope to episode and condition
	Full risk model	At the population and condition levels (the standard to have upside and downside risk)	More mature and includes PROMs, PREMs & clinician experience measures	The standard

Capitation

The population-based payment model most adopted in the initial transition from FFS to VBHC is called *capitation*. Providers are rewarded based on how their annual care costs compare to historical charges. In fully capitated systems, providers bear the cost difference between their capitation payments and actual expenses, with bonuses or penalties tied to meeting predefined metrics. There are two distinct advantages of capitation over FFS: it takes a population-based approach geared at outcomes rather than paying for individual procedures; and it fosters teamwork as both provider and payer co-create their joint incentives for the year.

This is recognized as a clear step forward on rebalancing the healthcare equation as, explained by Michael Porter and Robert Kaplan, because it *"rewards providers for lowering the overall cost of treating the entire population."*[84] However, they also outlined the limitations of such approach. Cost structures started gravitating with a bias *"toward generic high-cost areas, such as limiting the use of expensive tests and drugs, reducing readmissions, shortening lengths of stay, and discharging patients to their homes rather than to higher-cost rehabilitation facilities."* This hasn't always been to the greatest benefit of patients.

Therefore, although a step in the right direction, there are additional payment models that create even more opportunity for patient centricity, sharing risk, and creation value, while balancing outcomes with investments.

Bundled payments

Now, in my (Caitlin's) opinion, where payment models start to become more exciting is when we talk about *bundled* payments.

Having seen this work in my years working on payer-provider partnerships, bundles have since been gaining traction globally because
they focus on conditions and procedures that offer the most opportunity for cost reduction and quality improvement. By definition,
a bundled payment is a model where payments are made based on
a defined clinical episode of care, and there is a link between the
outcomes for improving quality and the cost of care. This model
offers flexibility because an episode of care can encompass a single
setting or bring together a full suite of services under one price,
and it can also define the episode across settings and services.

As an example, the Centers for Medicare and Medicaid Services
(CMS) in the US has successfully implemented bundles focused on
the post-acute space, such as Jim's hospital discharge after an AMI.
The Bundled Payments Care Improvement—Advanced (BPCI-A)
program for Medicare beneficiaries includes over thirty episodes of
care (based on inpatient and outpatient diagnoses and procedures)
and is focused on reducing cost in the ninety days post-discharge.
CMS (the payer) provides the necessary data for providers to
understand where their highest post-acute costs are within the
eligible episodes, and providers pick which episodes they will
participate in. Providers start intervening with patients while
they are still at the hospital ('inpatient') and start collaborating
with providers in the post-acute space, based on data provided to
them by CMS, on which providers (such as rehabilitation facilities,
specialized nursing facilities, or home health agencies) provide
the highest value care. Without data sharing across payer and
provider, this model would be impossible; the data CMS has is
key to setting up the program, the data the provider collects is
key to immediate and clear decision making, and then CMS must

share the full cost data post episode for the provider to have a full lens into their final performance. In the calendar year 2021, this model resulted in savings of 465 million dollars for Medicare, with an average of 930 dollars per episode, with redesign of activities changing the culture, relationships, and process across key players of the 5P, such as providers, payers, and patients.[88, 96]

Full risk

Across these different payment models, health care leaders are balancing the quandary of radically improving their cost structures, while keeping an eye on health care worker satisfaction and getting care delivery right for patients. This is all while aligning the complexity of metrics, connecting them to payments, and keeping the organization afloat. Hence, a new payment model that we refer to as the *"full risk model"* features "quality" instead of "quantity." To support its implementation and success, new metrics must include patient experience measures, staff satisfaction scores, process compliance indicators, and overall outcomes such as complication and readmission rates short- and mid-term as well as patient-reported outcomes (PROMs).[5, 77, 78]

2. Novel payment models in drug development

While the regular care delivery experience is revolutionary, the pharmaceutical and innovation sectors are also driving new approaches with payers to reimburse for new medicines.

The era of pushing drugs to the market at any price has seen a dead-end. Charging for products without evidence of sustained value for patients has been rejected by payers, health authorities, doctors, and patients for good reasons.

As introduced by Nienke in the previous chapter, we have seen novel collaborative value generation emerge most recently through innovative payment models that take a holistic look at the patient population sharing similar needs toward desired outcomes (figure 4.5).

Figure 4.5: Options on how drug developers can go about seeking VBC models.

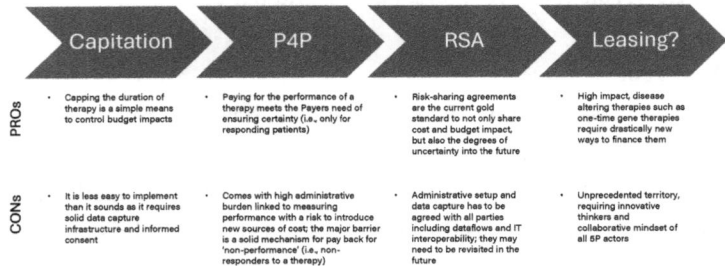

Capitation	P4P	RSA	Leasing?

	Capitation	P4P	RSA	Leasing?
PROs	• Capping the duration of therapy is a simple means to control budget impacts	• Paying for the performance of a therapy meets the Payers need of ensuring certainty (i.e., only for responding patients)	• Risk-sharing agreements are the current gold standard to not only share cost and budget impact, but also the degrees of uncertainty into the future	• High impact, disease altering therapies such as one-time gene therapies require drastically new ways to finance them
CONs	• It is less easy to implement than it sounds as it requires solid data capture infrastructure and informed consent	• Comes with high administrative burden linked to measuring performance with a risk to introduce new sources of cost; the major barrier is a solid mechanism for pay back for 'non-performance' (i.e., non-responders to a therapy)	• Administrative setup and data capture has to be agreed with all parties including dataflows and IT interoperability; they may need to be revisited in the future	• Unprecedented territory, requiring innovative thinkers and collaborative mindset of all 5P actors

In brief, and similar to the provider environment, *capitation* is a simple and effective way to manage budgets. *Pay-for-performance* (P4P) and *risk-sharing agreement* (RSA) models both account for the fact that a new medicine may not work for all patients equally and therefore has to include single outcome measurements. The former is strictly looking at the patient level and whether an individual patient derives benefit from a therapy or not—and parties will agree on the degree of reimbursement for each outcome stratification that is previously defined. The latter is the current "gold standard" as it transcends beyond single patient data assessments and takes a population stand. In this case, both parties—payer and pharma—will look at predefined, time-bound, population-based budget impacts over the years, and draw a line on increasing uncertainty and risk that is introduced with longer looks into the future. In simple terms, RSA is an envelope agreement in which both parties agree to a product price in a defined number of patients in a given year. If the threshold budget is surpassed, parties will agree on how to share the risk, aka who pays how much of the additional budget impact in the years to come.

Nienke already alluded to such a framework in the previous chapter, namely figure 3.4. To provide a telling example of the power of the 5Ps ability to shape new policy, let me share my (Verena's) own experience in Korea.

Back in 2010, Revlimid® was approved for second line treatment of patients with multiple myeloma, a therapy bringing about substantial improvement for what was a deadly outlook for patients at that time.[99] In Korea, where I took the medical director helm in 2011, no one questioned the clinical value of this therapy: doctors, patients, payers. However, the health authorities did not agree to its international price tag. Period. Long story short, after two years of bargaining, the negotiations stalled and the company was ready to pull the BATNA card (the *best alternative to a negotiated agreement,* one of the seven steps of MPC that Suzanne describes in the concluding chapter). Yet, there was a decisive and unforeseen turn of events before we were about to crash into a total lose-lose situation of not providing that treatment to Korean patients.

During a round table discussion, representatives from the company (medical and commercial), clinician key opinion leaders, and representatives of the ministry of health started moaning about the supposed failure in negotiation. Then one voice at the table said, *"Listen, we really liked what you put on the table: sharing the risk of the budget impact beyond two years with a gradual change of taking on overspending between the payer and the company. We've told you that we cannot entertain that option because we have no regulatory framework and no law to implement this upon. Now, given the new priorities of the president-elect putting cancer top of the country's agenda, I think we have a good chance to get the attention from parliament to actually pass a new bill."*[100]

This is why we say: value-based care is negotiation. Among all five actors.

It only takes a single person to speak up and challenge the status quo. That's all. Fast forward to today, the law and regulation on RSA is now a standing option for any new innovative medicine entering the Korean market.[101]

It showcases that no one actor alone is able to craft innovative solutions along the patient journey that meet everyone's needs and interests.

From capitation to P4P and RSA, all options have one basic theme in common: understanding deeply patients' needs and their holistic patient journey "beyond the pill."

With even further novel innovation coming to the market, such as cell-and-gene and gene therapies, carrying price tags of multiple millions, the entire concept of paying for drugs while curing diseases requires a deep revolutionary mindset. The old FFS system of paying cents and dollars for an aspirin cannot be the solution for a once-in-a-lifetime highly innovative therapy such as a gene modified injection curing a child from a deadly disease. More radical models, such as leasing or similar, will need to be designed in a collaborative dialogue between health care leaders representing the 5P perspectives, as well as society.

YES, WE CAN: PAYING FOR VALUE

The personal anecdote I (Caitlin) shared earlier proved that by removing silos between payers and the other 5P stakeholders, patient outcomes improve and health care costs are lowered. We now know there are a myriad of payment models available that can facilitate the alignment of care across different settings, ensuring the patient consistently remains at the center of care. As Verena and I noted, *VBHC is negotiation*, and it is through negotiation that the 5P actors will be able to fully move away from FFS to adopting these payment models as the standard.

Now, the question is: how can the other 5Ps enable the payer's success in driving higher value care and a successful tango?! Empowered *patients* speaking up, flagging that the status quo is no longer okay and requesting to be included in participative decisions, thus making health care delivery more affordable by only paying for outcomes that matter, including easier access to value-based preventive care. Collaborative *policymakers* have a tremendous opportunity to enable sandboxes for new models by taking a leadership role in designing them, developing regulatory frameworks for new funding models by fostering pilots, and catalyzing cooperation across all levels of the healthcare system—from executives to the clinical line staff. Participative *providers* becoming educated around payment models and VBHC, and supportive hospital administrators and CEOs to embark on novel payer-provider contracting. And, lastly, for *pharma*, finding innovative ways to share risks and pay for new breakthrough medications that allow shared value generation for all through reimbursement based on outcomes that matter to patients.

We have shown that payers have a tremendous opportunity to align with all other actors along the 5P value chain to bridge silos. By working together, all gain a clear pathway to align incentives and work toward a common goal.

Before we move on, payers can first understand where their cost
and quality challenges lie by reflecting on the following questions.

- **Population:** What group of patients with which medical condition
  with similar needs do I prioritize? How do I marry the data on
  which conditions to prioritize to the anecdotal data from patients,
  providers, and payers?

- **Waste identification:** How can I analyze the data I hold and
  identify the top three issues in the cost structure likely causing (in)
  efficiencies? Are there areas of low-value care that drive unnecessary cost?

- **Patient journey:** Can I draw the patient journey from start to finish
  and identify redundancies, gaps, and areas for both clinical and
  societal aspects that contribute to better outcomes?

- **Future state care pathway:** Can I co-create the future by selecting
  and prioritizing the pathways where providers are most focused
  and then garner feedback? Who else outside of my own silo do I
  need? Policy? Patients? Hospitals?

- **Best practices:** What other precedents can I learn from to help
  craft my analysis? Other countries, other regions, other cities?
  What worked for these precedents, and what didn't work? What is
  the best starting point to gain traction?

CHAPTER 5

The *Policymaker* view on supporting patient centricity and care coordination

By Paul Sherrington

*"Unacknowledged dependencies remain the
number one cause of project slippage. The cure
is lateral, cross-functional connectivity."*

~ JOHN DOERR

I have spent most of my life working in the field of blood cancers, initially doing basic research and running a diagnostics lab in an academic medical center in the UK, and later followed by many years in the pharmaceutical company sector. My exposure to health authorities and their policies in the earlier part of my life was confined to that of a passive consumer of UK health care, probably just like most other citizens. It was only later during my pharma years that I really started to gain some global exposure on the role and creation of regulatory environments for health care. As a medical department pharma representative, I was involved in several meetings negotiating access to novel therapies and medicines with government-related bodies such as the National Institute for Health and Care Excellence (NICE), which is the healthcare policy-shaping body in the UK.

HEALTHCARE SYSTEMS:
TRANSCENDING BUREAUCRACY

In public opinion, health authorities carry somewhat of a poor image, just like any government-related agency does nowadays.

I always wondered how such a bureaucratic shining body like an EMA or FDA (the European and US medicine agencies respectively), with their long lists of laws and regulations, would actually facilitate research and care. Entire departments and role descriptions flank pharma companies and hospital administrations only to comply with rules, regulations, quality reports, and pharmacovigilance reporting lists. One study found that physicians spent twice as much time on paperwork as they did with patients.[1] How does this reconcile with what the agencies' foundational purpose is, namely, to ensure the safe and appropriate use of medicines in human beings?

For many, dealing with health authorities is a transactional relationship and a necessary evil on the way to get treatments or clinical trials approved with a service-provider mentality. The idea of it being a collaboration anchored in common purpose—or even a strategic partnership—is not something that is part of daily jobs as a regulatory or market access person working in pharma, MedTech, or as a clinical researcher in an academic medical center.

Figure 5.1: The question remains: How to manage bureaucracy and overwhelming bodies of regulations in clinical research and regular care delivery to ensure both innovation and safe therapies for patients?

In the 1980s, due to a family history of hypertension, I was referred to a cardiology clinic for some routine assessments (or so I thought!). During this clinic visit, I was told that I would be followed for the rest of my life as part of a clinical trial if I was to be prescribed an antihypertensive drug. Even without knowing anything about the regulations governing clinical research and obviously without knowing what I know now, I was quite taken aback by this statement. Especially as there was no discussion about whether I *wanted* to take part in that trial and what it would entail! I think, back then, I imagined information about me being used in circumstances under which I had no control.

I didn't want to be labeled as a sick person.

At that point in my life, I had never heard of a *consent form*, or, worse, was never offered one. In the end, I didn't agree to get into that trial and I wasn't prescribed that drug. So, I eventually forgot all about it. Until recently, as I was starting to reflect on the content for this chapter.

Luckily, there have been enormous changes since the 1980s with regard to patient involvement in any form of clinical research. To date, it would be unheard of to suggest to someone that they would be followed as part of a clinical trial without a description of what that trial entails, its aims, and the expectations of the individual volunteering/agreeing to take part. No clinical research center would get away with not offering an *informed consent form* (ICF) ensuring no concerns about privacy or confidentiality of my data.

When Verena and Hanna approached me to contribute to this *Next Tango*, it became quickly clear to me that I wanted to share my personal experience navigating healthcare policy, in addition to my professional experiences with it over the past decades, for your benefit as a reader.

THE ROLE OF THE POLICYMAKER

Health care is one of the most, if not *the* most, regulated industry.

Rightly so, as we are dealing with human lives. In health care, the ultimate customer is the patient. As outlined in Verena's first book, *TangoForFive*, the historical making of policy bodies dates back to the 1960s.[1] Both on the product development side of things, which drives innovation in medicine, as well as the regular care delivery reality of providers and patients, these acts and transactions must be tightly regulated. As Caitlin and Verena alluded to in the previous chapter, various countries got themselves organized in different ways, harmonized like the EMA for the European member states, or nationalized like the FDA in the US and NICE in the UK (for ample reading on country peculiarities of health authorities in a sample of eleven countries, I recommend reading Dr Zeke Emanuel's landmark book, *Which Country Has the World's Best Health Care?*).[102]

Healthcare policies are made by multiple organizations, or even individuals, ranging from global organizations like the WHO, national governments, regional governmental bodies, NGOs, healthcare insurers, hospitals, health technology assessment (HTA) bodies, pharmaceutical companies, patients' and advocacy groups, and individual general practitioners.

Of note, and for the purpose of clarity in this book, I solely confine the discussion to the major players with the biggest influence on the provision of health care to patients, such as policies in the context of clinical research and digital health matters, and won't go into details here on healthcare compliance-type regulations (e.g. data protection).

A COORDINATED PATH TO POLICY

I am wondering, though, whether this mysterious black box of ever-increasing regulations and policies can still be reconciled with a patient-centric lens on the primary purpose of safeguarding human health.[103, 104]

For this, I went ahead and looked at our previous chapters and summarized some topline concerns and hurdles that I've noticed— and that actually get in the way of making a more collaborative and strategic partnership with health authorities a reality (figure 5.2). "You can't treat what you didn't diagnose," as the saying goes, and to stay within the medical metaphors here.

Being highly interdependent but yet acting more often than not in silos, the daily realities can jeopardize health care leaders to keep their best intentions on the north of what's best for the patient.

All actors along the 5P value chain that are developing and delivering health care must operate within this ethical and regulatory framework.

Figure 5.2: Interests and constraints for each actor to deliver patient-centric results in health care.

5P-Actor	Interests and Policy Constraints to Stay Patient-Centric
Policymakers and Governments	• Keeping the population healthy (public health matters, pandemics, vaccines) • Balancing budgets within economic frameworks and other national interests • Deciding on which therapies and drugs will gain access and at what price
Payers and Health insurances	• Paying for the care and medicines whilst not owning the product pricing decisions • Negotiating terms of reimbursement for formularies with policy and providers
Providers and Hospital systems	• Prescribers determine which procedure and product is given to the patient • Doctors have a freedom of decision-making for what the best medical choice is
Pharma, MedTech and the Life Sciences	• Bringing products to the market through marketing authorization approval (MAA) and ensure ROIs for shareholders to sustain finances • Reconciling the evidence from a narrow patient population in clinical trials into the broad real-life population of a country that is required by the payer
Patients	• Fix my Problem: Getting affordable access to the best treatment fast

Health authorities and their policymakers across the world are subscribed to government oversight. Its commissioners and main decision makers undergo election cycles just as their politician bosses do. That being said, their primary goal is to safeguard public health, and fight pandemics and other communicable diseases, and oversee prevention programs such as vaccination and other health threats stemming from the environment and natural habitat of a country. In order to implement those principles, they issue laws and regulations governing providers and payers. In many countries, the health authorities play the role of gatekeeping decision making on which novel treatments and drugs will be allowed in the country. All of the European markets have such HTA bodies and many of them also govern the price tag that will be attributed to these products. (For more detail, I refer the interested reader to the annually updated W.A.I.T.—Waiting to Access Innovative Therapies—Indicator.)[105]

Policymakers must balance the competing interests of the other players. Pharmaceutical companies face challenges in managing income generation with drug development costs, often resorting to lobbying to influence policy decisions. Providers, including healthcare systems and physicians, face ethical dilemmas weighing patient care against the financial constraints imposed on them. They contribute to healthcare policymaking by sharing expertise and influencing decisions at various levels. Health care payers, such as insurers and government programs, influence policies to control costs and ensure access to services. They are pivotal in shifting healthcare systems toward VBC models. Payers impact reimbursement models, cost efficiency, and quality-based care delivery through various strategies and initiatives. Patients and advocacy groups are, nevertheless, increasingly influencing healthcare policies by participating in policy development, influencing research, promoting equity and access, advocating for ethical standards, supporting digital health, collaborating with stakeholders, ensuring accountability, and by monitoring policy implementation.

*Patients' involvement is crucial in creating
patient-centered healthcare systems.*

As we learned in great detail in the previous chapter, health insurers and health plans pay for the care and medicines. In most markets, they are however not the ones setting the price of a procedure or a pill. This is governed by the lawmaker and its representatives such as the HTA bodies. A tight negotiation on what should get listed, and at what price and under which conditions, is therefore a prime intersection that is not always without friction and tension.

One of the biggest burning issues is the intersection between the doctors' freedom to prescribe according to their professional oath and the regulatory product labels and the reimbursement conditions. Evidence-based medicine is the commonly referred standard for doctors who have spent years at medical schools and clinical fellowships to identify the best possible care plan for a patient based on all the available scientific standards to do so. Entire medical congresses are catering to tens of thousands of doctors each year to share those scientific advances. However, the seven hurdles of drug development are a lengthy endeavor to bring these new innovations to the market: to the patient (figure 3.1).[1] Practically speaking, the latest W.A.I.T. indicator reported continued delays in access for patients with a staggering drug availability in approved indications of only forty-three per cent in Europe, and an average time of 531 (!) days until novel medicines are available to patients—aka being paid for.[105]

Despite the best education for doctors, they aren't
always able to prescribe what the scientific data for
best outcomes say—and—hence patients are not
always receiving the best therapy as per evidence
because they are not reimbursed nor paid for yet.

However, the good news is that doctors and provider systems are stepping up and are becoming more and more proactive (see the breakout box below). Healthcare systems, hospitals, physicians, and other HCPs influence healthcare policymaking through their expertise, advocacy, and direct involvement in policy formulation. By collaborating with government agencies, contributing data and evidence, and lobbying for sustainable health care models, they ensure that policies reflect the realities of care delivery while advancing patient care, quality standards, and system-wide improvements. Their role is crucial for creating healthcare policies that balance the needs of patients, providers, and the broader health system.

HOSPITAL AND HEALTH SYSTEM
PARTICIPATION IN POLICY INITIATIVES

Large healthcare systems often lead the way in advocating for policies that align with integrated care models, where health care delivery is more coordinated, and patient outcomes are prioritized. They influence policies that are aimed at coordinated health care delivery (avoiding fragmentation), improving coordination between hospitals, primary care, and specialty services.[106, 107]

They also actively participate in pilot programs and experimental initiatives launched by governments or regulatory bodies to test new health care models, such as accountable care organizations (ACOs) or bundled payment models (see Chapter 4).

The results of these programs often inform future policy decisions, particularly in areas like cost containment, efficiency, and patient-centered care.

Pharmaceutical drug developers, and nowadays, tech companies developing innovative tools and devices to treat cancer and other diseases, are facing a harsh barrier of market entry both with health authorities such as FDA and EMA as well as HTA bodies such as NICE and other payer bodies. One of the toughest hurdles to climb isn't necessarily to gain a marketing authorization approval (MAA). But what I have observed and discussed many times in my joint years with Verena in drug development is that regulators and payers have opposing interests when it comes to the patient population required.

Regulators require the most narrowly described patient population while the payer requires a real-world body of data that the new pill actually works in the entire population with this disease in a particular country.

In practical terms: regulatory authorities who are issuing the MAA want to see the results from a subgroup of patients. Let's assume a hypothetical example of a clinical study investigating a promising black pill for cancer of the big toe, with restricted study eligibility criteria that only enroll the younger, wealthy, and well-educated patients. All because their task is to draw a reliable assessment without confounding biases of this black pill's *risk-benefit ratio*. In other words, unwanted side effects like stomach bleeding versus its potential for cure. On the other hand, the other authorities eventually *paying* for this black pill need to ensure that *all* the others that were excluded from the study, such as the less well informed, the poor, and the old living with cancer of the big toe also have a demonstrated benefit of the treatment. A tension that often requires the submission of two different datasets to two different health authorities comprising diverging sets of patient data. I'll get back to this shortly.

WHAT ARE THE INTERESTS OF THE PATIENT?

Well, in this noisy technical and regulatory environment, of which I've only been scratching the surface, the patients' interests—getting the best possible care, fast—are not always met to their satisfaction.[105]

In recent years, patients and advocacy groups have taken on an increasingly influential role in the development of healthcare policies.[108] Their participation has become critical as healthcare systems aim to become more patient-centered, focusing on the needs, preferences, and outcomes that matter most to those receiving care. Here are some insights on five select areas, in which individual patients as well as patient advocacy groups are shaping policies.

1. A voice in policymaking and legislative advocacy

Patients and advocacy groups now regularly participate in policy discussions at both the national and local levels. Their involvement ensures that policies are not just based on clinical or economic considerations but also reflect the real-world experiences of patients.

Many patient groups work directly with lawmakers and parliament to advocate for laws that improve access to care, fund research, or protect patient rights. For instance, groups advocating for rare diseases often lobby for more research funding or expedited drug approvals.

Stemming from the French-speaking territories, the *"partenariat patients"* concept has become widespread, with initiatives in Canada, France, Switzerland, and the UK.[109, 110]

2. Shaping research and drug development

Patients are increasingly involved not just as "subjects" in clinical trials but as active collaborators, as you've read in great detail in Chapter 2 and also mentioned by Nienke from a pharma perspective (figure 3.2). Patients actively help design trials that are more relevant to the right patient population (according to the three-step VBHC process shown in figure 1.6) by collecting and measuring relevant patient experiences, increasing patients' participation and adherence to study procedures, and ultimately ensuring that only outcomes that matter to patients are measured, such as the utilization of PROMs and PREMs.

Advocacy groups have generally pushed for greater patient involvement also in shaping the strategy of clinical research agendas. This has led to the rise of patient-centered outcomes research (PCOR), where patients help determine which outcome tools and methodology (e.g., quality of life, ease of treatment) are most important to a given clinical trial.[60, 110, 111]

In some regions, regulatory bodies like the US FDA or the EMA in Europe have introduced formal mechanisms for including patient input into the MAA process.[112, 113] To my observation, this has helped prioritize treatments for diseases with high unmet needs tremendously.

3. Leveraging real-world data

As showcased in my example of cancer of the big toe, payers usually request much wider patient populations, just like they occur in the real world, outside of a skewed patient population eligible only within clinical trials as required by the regulator. Over the past decade, this has led to increasing support for using real-word evidence (RWE) datasets as a critical step toward more inclusive representation of all individuals living with a certain medical condition.

Regulations driven by the FDA on the use of such real-world data (RWD), collected from regular patient charts, claims data, and disease registries, is one of my highlights of progress in recent years.[114]

It is encouraging to me to see that patients and advocacy groups increasingly work with pharmaceutical companies to co-create solutions—as also outlined by Nienke and Hanna in their respective chapters. This may include working together on designing patient-friendly treatment regimens or developing patient assistance programs to help with the cost of medications.

4. Promoting equity and access

Coming back to a topic that was briefly introduced in Chapter 2, many advocacy groups increasingly focus on health disparities, fighting for better access to care for underrepresented groups such as low-income populations, racial and ethnic minorities, and people living with disabilities. These groups have been instrumental in pushing policies that include SDOH parameters and therefore ensure broader health care coverage.

Patients and their advocates have been vocal in debates about health insurance policies, advocating for coverage expansions, reduced out-of-pocket costs, and protections for individuals with pre-existing conditions. This was particularly prominent during discussions around the Affordable Care Act (ACA) in the US.[115, 116]

5. Literacy, digital health, and health technology

Last, but not least, the patient voice with regard to digital health is paramount. With widespread access to the internet, wearables, and smart devices, the patient becomes a real custodian of their own data—just as Hanna has done with her own condition (as highlighted in Chapter 1).

With the rise of digital health technologies, patient advocacy groups have pushed for regulations that ensure these tools are accessible, affordable, and secure. Patients have also become strong advocates for better control over how their health data is used, particularly in the context of AI and big data. They have emphasized the need for transparency, consent, and the ethical use of personal health information.[117-120]

*In summary, patients and patient advocacy groups
have moved from being passive recipients of care to
active participants in healthcare policy development.*

By advocating for patient-centered approaches, influencing research priorities, promoting equitable access, and pushing for accountability, patients play a critical role in shaping the future of healthcare systems globally. This is not a new concept. Let me share a historical example and a more recent example showcasing how patient engagement can effectively lead to shaping new policies.

In the 1980s, the advocacy group National Organization for Rare Disorders (NORD) successfully lobbied for the passage of the Orphan Drug Act (1983) in the US.[121] This act provides financial incentives for pharmaceutical companies to develop treatments for rare diseases, which otherwise might be ignored due to small market size.

More recently, advocacy groups of the T1D international society, under the chaperon of the American Diabetes Association (ADA), have brought attention to the rising costs of insulin (particularly in the US), that life-saving drug for people with diabetes. Through grassroots efforts and campaigns, these groups have effectively pressured lawmakers to address insulin price gouging.[122]

MAKING IT REAL: NEW POLICY
FRAMEWORKS FOR PATIENT CENTRICITY

I have represented two different companies at the English HTA organization, NICE, to negotiate new drugs for reimbursement. Each time I was facing these health authority officials, I had the slight feeling I was being viewed with suspicion. I felt like I was under the microscope as someone who just wanted the company to make money. In reality, I only ever wanted patients to have access to the most appropriate treatments. I echo Nienke's observation in the sense that black sheep exist everywhere. However, these days, I believe most people in this sector generally have patients in mind, always.

Wouldn't it be good in turn if all the actors involved in shaping, creating, and pushing healthcare policy could just trust each other to have the end user, the patient, at heart, always?

Figure 5.3: Who is the committee? Who decides? Shouldn't it be a collaborative effort between patients, providers, pharma, payers, and policymakers?

"The Committee's decided to ban further research until it can be proven your 'wheel' poses no threat to the environment, society or public health."

I've always felt strongly that I wanted to work in an area that benefits society. After spending many years thinking I was doing just that, by contributing to the wealth of knowledge on hematologic malignancies on the bench, albeit in a very small way, I went to work in the pharmaceutical sector thinking that as part of the medical affairs team I could still contribute in a positive way. Slightly to my surprise, I believe I did more to benefit patients with blood cancers in these roles than I did by conducting basic research.

The good news is to see a plethora of patient-centric work being done by health authorities.

The list is actually too long to be captured in this chapter, hence I am only selecting a few in figure 5.4 to demonstrate the point that health authorities are not only that perceived black box of administrative writers of laws, regulations, and policies, but actually have evolved in recent years into strategic thinkers, collaborators, and drivers of innovation in and of itself.

Figure 5.4: Examples of health policies driving research and implementation of patient-centric care improvements.

Region	Policy	Date	Description	Relevance
Europe	European Health Data Space (EHDS)[118]	Proposed in 2022	Aims to create a common space for health data in the EU, allowing for better patient access, use of health data for research, and harmonization of data standards.	Facilitates patient control over their health data and enhances cross-border healthcare services.
	EU Artificial Intelligence (AI) Act[119]	Proposed in 2021, ongoing	Categorizes AI systems based on risk, and sets specific regulations for AI in health care, ensuring safety, transparency, and accountability in AI-based health applications.	Important for developers and users of AI in health care to comply with safety and ethical standards.
	The EU Data Governance Act[120]	Adopted in 2022	Establishes a framework for data sharing across the EU, with particular emphasis on non-personal and anonymized health data for research and innovation.	Encourages the use of health data for innovation while ensuring privacy and security.
	EU health technology assessment (HTA) regulation[123]	Starts January 2025	Aims to streamline the evaluation of health technologies to improve the accessibility of innovative therapies. First focus is on oncology treatments and advanced therapies.	Provides a centralized process for scientific assessments, covering clinical aspects (efficacy and safety), which can be used by national health authorities.
	EFPIA— W.A.I.T. indicator[105]	Published June 2024	2023 survey comprising thirty-six countries, including all EU27 countries.	Indicators measure availability, including limited availability and time taken to reimburse in each member state.
	UK blood cancer charity initiatives[124, 125]	Started 2019	The Blood Cancer UK Policy Panel was established so that people affected by blood cancer are at the center of government and NHS decision making.	Highlighting the incidence of blood cancers in the UK to raise awareness and push for governmental policies to enable research and funding for new treatments.
		July 2024	Leukaemia UK called for the new government to commit to and publish a fully funded cancer strategy within the first year.	
	SAKK Patient and Public Involvement (PPI)[110, 111]	Started 2022	1st international workshop on PPI in cancer research by SAKK (Schweizerische Arbeitsgemeinschaft für Klinische Krebsforschung).	Active programs to co-create novel study designs between clinician researchers and patients.

Region	Policy	Date	Description	Relevance
USA	21st Century Cures Act— Information Blocking Rule[117]	Enforced in 2021	Prohibits practices that prevent patients from accessing their electronic health information; mandates that patients have full access to their health records through standardized application programming interfaces (APIs).	Empowers patients by ensuring they have timely and secure access to their health data.
	ONC's Final Rule on Interoperability and Patient Access[126]	Enforced in 2021	Requires HCPs to adopt standardized APIs for patient access to health information, facilitating easier data exchange and patient control.	Promotes interoperability and enhances patient access to their own health data across different systems.
	FDA Real-World Evidence (RWE) Framework 2021[114]	Started 2021	Real-world data (RWD) use in regulatory decision making.	Encourages the use of RWE in supporting drug and device MAA, including post-marketing.
	Center for Biologics Evaluation and Research (CBER) and Center for Drug Evaluation and Research (CDER) real-world evidence[127]	Proposed 2024	The International Council for Harmonisation (ICH) released a reflection paper titled "Pursuing Opportunities for Harmonisation in Using Real-World Data (RWD) to Generate RWE, with a focus on Effectiveness of Medicines."	The ultimate goal of this initiative is to further enable the integration of RWE in regulatory submissions and timely regulatory decision making.

Healthcare policies in particular and medicine in general are shaped by a complex web of interactions involving policymakers, patients, providers, payers, and pharmaceutical companies. Pulling back the curtain of partisan perceptions offers a deeper understanding of the motivations that influence each stakeholder group. As the health care environment continues to evolve, choreographing the negotiation and collaboration between these key dance partners could provide the selective pressure to drive a continually evolving enhancement of global health.

⚑ ☆	POLICYMAKER REFLECTION BOX ON PATIENT CENTRICITY

Supporting patient centricity was a key focus in this chapter. Before we move on, here are some questions to consider in relation to policy shaping.

- **Literacy:** What is my experience in health care in general? Which group do I belong to in the 5Ps? Is there something in my area I can make a difference with and what do I need to learn about policy initiatives to do so?

- **Information:** Can I get informed about possible initiatives in my vicinity—my town, my region, my country, or within my disease community? Does my doctor know anything more about policy shaping and how I could contribute?

- **Involvement:** Is there a PPI/PPIE group in my country, region, or disease community that I can get involved in and raise my voice concerning policy shaping or clinical trials?

- **Politics:** Do I use my vote in elections covering health care topics? Am I aware of lawmakers covering healthcare policy in my national and city elections or any referenda put forward?

- **Peer group:** Is there a group I could join (i.e. in my preferred social media channels)?

THE 6TH P

The fabric of dancing a collaborative tango in health care

By Suzanne Robinson and Verena Voelter

*"The key point is not to focus on the
wall, but to transcend it."*

~ ZEEV NEUWIRTH

In the previous chapter, Paul Sherrington got straight to the point: interests and constraints for actors to stay patient-centric.

It seems that we are not lacking great ideas, nor great initiatives to break down silos and develop more patient-centric health care. However, as you are coming off reading the five perspectives of the key actors dancing an entwined tango in health care, you may be thinking, "That's all great—but how is this going to work?" Many people these days are calling out for a neutral platform and some mysterious unknown person or entity that will adjudicate all these varying interests, positions, and opinions. "Who is the 6th P?" we are often asked.

Well, sorry to tell you this, but there isn't one.

Although there are great independent bodies that foster collaborative value creation across the 5Ps, to use an orchestra analogy, there really is no *one* conductor who would sit above those other five first violinists. In this final chapter, we are proposing a song sheet that has proven to catalyze teamwork across all actors required to achieve best possible health care. That is, the previously described seven-step framework to *multi-party collaboration* (MPC).[1] We are refreshing it here with new examples and real-life guides for you to start trying it out in your own day-to-day reality.

THE SONG SHEET TO COLLABORATION

The good news is that much of the collaborative work required by each and every party to break down barriers across the complex health care sector has already started. As Dr Zeev Neuwirth states in his latest book, *Beyond The Walls*, the humanistic movement of entrepreneurs in health care is already happening as he recounts ample examples where the "*mindset, the spirit, and the actions of trailblazing leaders and organizations*" have already brought fresh winds into new ways of working.[128]

Figure 6.1: Two or more parties working together toward a common goal creates value.

Unfortunately, *"there are not many natural-born negotiators"* equipped with the tools to integrate all perspectives toward one solution, as stated by the Program on Negotiation (PON) team at Harvard Law School.[1]

Negotiation here is defined as a way for two people to reach an agreement on how to work together toward a joint goal. That's what the seven steps of MPC provide: a set of common vocabulary and processes enabling the five actors in health care to propel change in a systematic and scalable fashion.

Many of our partners and clients have embraced this MPC framework, as it puts the sharing and understanding of mutual interests

front and center in the process. We will weave these steps into this
concluding chapter as we recap our learnings from this *Next Tango*.

Bringing together all actors of the value chain around the proverbial round table means all health care leaders stepping up to
the plate. No matter where you sit at that table—as a doctor,
pharma executive, health insurer, government official, patient, or
consultant—it is paramount we all start hearing out each actor's
needs, pressures, and obligations. Once you start capturing some
of the intricacies of each other's needs and business pressures, by
removing that curtain just a little bit more (figure ii), you come to
appreciate the complexity of each one's daily reality.

Hence, we were struck by Caitlin's summary as she was walking
out of our 2023 5P Flagship Event, which featured some of the
finest professional negotiators and tango dancers on stage. *"Of
course, it's obvious,"* she told us. *"Why wasn't I thinking of this
earlier? Aligning the interests of payers, providers, and patients is
nothing but a negotiation."*[70]

Originally stemming out of the area of conflict resolution at Harvard Law School, you may recall that Roger Fisher first introduced
this song sheet of interest-based negotiation some fifty years ago in
his landmark book, *Getting to Yes*.[129] Meanwhile, after many years of
adopting this framework ourselves in health care, we have evolved
its description to *multi-party collaboration*, as the clear objective
is to avoid frank and noisy conflict by getting ahead of the curve
and finding a resolution before the point of no return is reached.

Aligning *interests*. This is a great way to consider Getting *Past
No*—the title of William Ury's follow-on book on negotiation.[130]

A "no" can be delivered and received with inadvertent conflict in the same way as giving a "yes" too soon can set up for disappointment. In this section, we talk about the required steps to effective negotiation: a framework to enable both you and the other party (or parties) to walk away with at least what you intended to achieve (if not more), all of which is anchored in a strong sense of value while keeping your relationships intact and even strengthening them, facilitating future engagements.

Figure 6.2: The seven steps of multi-party collaboration (MPC) built on a common purpose and fueled by curiosity. In other words, moving from lose-lose value destruction to win-win collaborative value creation.

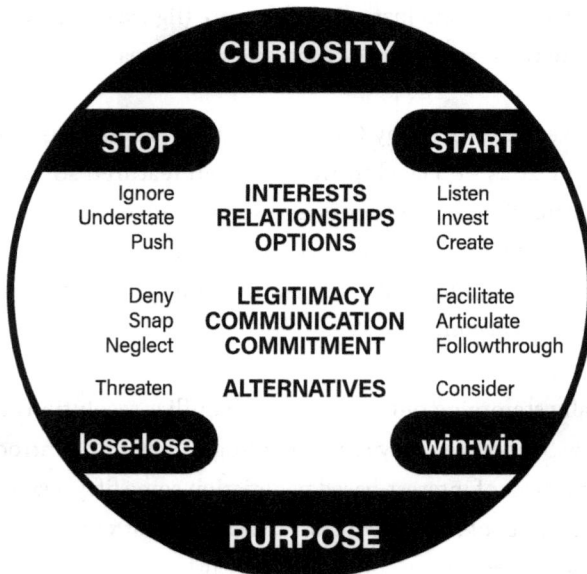

Before we discuss further how MPC can propel patient centricity into real-world health care, let's pause for a minute and hear a personal anecdote from Suzanne about her foray into the world of health care, negotiation, and collaboration.

BREAKING DOWN WALLS
THROUGH A COMMON PURPOSE

I first met Verena in 2010. Initially we were working on different diseases for the same pharma company, like "passing ships" due to our seemingly different interests. However, our common *purpose* was strong: working to fight cancer—"the big C." Verena's experience as an accomplished oncologist was somewhat intimidating to my younger self. It was only later that I realized my own expertise, beyond the science, as having been a carer and relative of someone battling cancer. More on this later. At a similar time, Verena and I joined the same disease team and, in doing so, we got to know one another by being curious, asking questions, and listening to one another's stories and underlying motivations to work in the fight against cancer. In turn, this has led to an understanding and appreciation of each other's beliefs, perceptions, and skills. By investing time in the *relationship*, we created a solid foundation of trust on which to cooperate together. And here we are, fifteen years later, writing a book together.

As a scientist and rational thinker, I have spent almost twenty-five years in the pharmaceutical industry, from big pharma to small biotech, within medical affairs across oncology and hematology. It was likely my encounter with the big C at age nineteen, when my mom was diagnosed with aggressive lymphoma, that unconsciously drove me to choose a career in cancer research and drug development. Nearly half of us will be affected by cancer during our lifetime. My own experience perhaps gave my younger self that purpose that I continue to follow today, whereby I continually ask myself: What contribution can I make?[131]

We turned to complementary medicine
so my mom could feel participative in her
treatment and regain a sense of control.

This was the 1990s, long before the internet made information available at our fingertips. It was before so-called targeted therapies, which nowadays can fight cancer like precision weapons. It was the time when "ugly" chemotherapy was the only mainstay. A one-size-fits-all toxic approach to treatment with a devastating plethora of side effects. My mom's prognosis was earth-shattering—one month to live! Today, a lot is spoken about quality of life (QoL) and we've heard from Hanna about tools such as PROMs and PREMs, meaning involvement in the care, enabling people diagnosed with a chronic condition to live a life worth living, on their own terms.

With the available cancer treatments thirty-five years ago, including a bone marrow transplant, my mom survived eighteen months. Both then and today, I think this is too short! I use the word "survived" here intentionally. While there were moments she felt well, and we even managed a surprise trip to Paris, most of her remaining time was spent either receiving treatment in hospital, or bedridden at home, managing the side effects of treatment, too weak to enjoy time with family and feeling miserable. My mom felt out of control of what was happening to her body. Treatment was decided by someone else, it was happening to her rather than with her, and the side effects hit like a bus—this is just the way it was—and so she became a pawn in her own health care. Luckily, thanks to the participative methods described by our co-authors

in Chapter 2, we regained some sense of control, and my mom
regained some of her self-esteem.

STEPPING UP WITH CURIOSITY

With the current advancements in science and technology,
thankfully chemotherapy is no longer the "norm" but part of a
wide-ranging armamentarium, including cell and gene therapies, in
the fight against cancer. Fortunately for other patients, the curve
of cancer mortality started bending shortly after my mom passed
away.[1, 132, 133] This is likely related to technological and scientific
advances, which in large part are due to phenomenal new ways of
collaborating across sectors in novel PPPs and co-creation between
academic and pharmaceutical research.[1] Curious and courageous
individuals on every side of the siloed fences are making these
breakthroughs happen (more on this soon).

Recently, we have seen another vivid example of such PPPs bending another curve: that of the COVID-19 pandemic, which led to
the rapid introduction of vaccines in less than one year. How was
this possible? It all started with that common *purpose* across the
five main actors in health care. The house was on fire, so to speak,
with people dying of this new bug even in the best healthcare
systems around the world. In clinical research, it usually takes
more than a decade and more than a billion dollars to bring a
new medicine to the market (as highlighted earlier in figure 3.1)!

The question is: how can we replicate these advances and bring
further innovation and improved care to patients in a consistent

manner? How can we avoid traps and conflict around unresolved diverging interests? How can the policy-related constraints described by Paul in Chapter 5 be managed consistently? How can providers and patients co-create in a participatory fashion as described by Hanna and the Claudias in chapters 1 and 2? What role can pharma play in a sustainable manner to dance a collaborative tango in health care, as Nienke told us about in Chapter 3? And how can payer-provider and payer-pharma partnerships be modeled toward a sustainable future, as Caitlin and Verena outlined in Chapter 4?

In brief, how can we ensure all actors appreciate the enhanced value they can create by engaging differently, *"listening, allowing everyone to express their grievance, untackling conflicts thanks to a joint work of mediation,"* as Béatrice Schaad and her co-authors summarize in the recent landmark book about conflict mediation in health care, *(In)hospitalités hospitalières.*[134]

Illustrated in figure 6.2, the seven-step MPC framework—anchored in a common purpose and fueled by curiosity—equips all actors along the patient-centric value chain with that common song sheet, so that they can co-create better care each and every time they come together.

We are all likely to be a patient at some point in our lives. Then many of us will want to understand what to expect, be listened to, and explore different treatment options. We will want to express our needs and interests.

We will want to understand the intent and interests of our care team and of those with whom we interact, wanting to be part of a shared decision-making process. This is true whether in the context of co-creating the treatment journey between patient and doctor, as Hanna outlined to us, or when designing joint care pathways between payers and providers or pharma, as described by Caitlin. After all, patients are the "paying customers" of their health care, whether directly or indirectly.

A case in point is how effective listening works in practice. When we make any other purchase—be it that handbag or pair of shoes for self-care—we can often observe the behavior pattern with the retail staff we encounter. In a shoe shop, for example, the top performing sales assistant does it to perfection: engaging with the customer (the *relationship*); asking questions about the customer's preferences (*interests*); inquiring if the shoes are for a special occasion (*purpose*); articulating the benefits of each shoe (*communication*); brainstorming together with the customer on various designs, sizes, and colors (*options*).

MOVING FROM SILOS TO CO-CREATION

Translating this back to medicine and health care, I am wondering how all the modern therapies could have shaped a different path for my mom. The innovations we have in cancer care today enable more patients to live *with* rather than survive *from* their diagnosis, having a much larger impact. But how do we ensure resources are in the right place at the right time for the right patient to balance the scales of innovation and access?

Current systems often reward a siloed approach, as referred to in earlier chapters. Each actor is laser-focused on their own interests, which in turn leads to misalignments lacking evidence or *legitimacy*, serving the *interests* of a single "P" only. Legitimacy, and the facts we base our perspectives on, can be the key to accessing a seemingly blocked avenue (refer to cost and risk-sharing models in Chapter 4) and ultimately facilitate a multi-party agreement. In the absence of a common purpose, we may deny the legitimacy of others to benefit ourselves. Keeping the patient at the center of our initial attempt is often a challenge.

From my experience of having been a carer and working in the pharmaceutical industry for many years, I see a lot of "talk" about patient centricity. However, the reality of siloed working and misaligned incentives too often leads to a one-size-fits-all approach, fueling inefficiencies and cost. A real lose-lose situation. To overcome this zero-sum game, it often needs more than one health care specialist around the proverbial round table at the same time as the patient. The silos in which the different health care specialists operate often block access to that table before conversations have even begun. When access is granted, the parties often focus on what is *not* possible rather than being creative and thinking of what *is* possible (see figure 6.3). For sure, the progress in medicine I've referred to since my mom passed wouldn't have been possible with people sticking to old behaviors.

Silos in health care are nothing new. What is new is the momentum across the 5P community to break down the walls that separate our functions.

So, what have we learned? The move toward more win-win situations that create value can only commence once we start *communicating* more. This means engaging with the other "Ps" as individuals, and showing *curiosity* about those with whom we negotiate, to listen, gain insights, and develop an understanding of the other people's *purpose*. What is important to them in their roles and in their lives? This could be as simple as asking, "Hey doc, why are you late? You look exhausted—having a tough day?" Or, "Hey, I'd really like to better understand what triggers that pain and maybe what alleviates it. Tell me more." As I said before, it comes down to listening—and wondering what the underlying beliefs, perceptions, motivations, experiences, challenges, and pressures are. "Do I really understand those payers' obligations? What are their budgets and what leeway do they have? Can I ask?"

Figure 6.3: Talk about options and solutions rather than hurdles and barriers.

"Can't we first discuss *objectives* before we're knee-deep in *objections?*"

By taking the time to get to know the other person, we are investing in our *relationship*. It is the most important measure to break through the big unknown bubble behind the curtain (figure ii). In both my and Verena's experience as negotiation coaches in health care, we often come across instances where leaders don't actually talk to the right person. Digging through the web of stakeholders in a company, organization or institution is time well spent. As Verena wrote in *TangoForFive*, "*organizations are made of people.*"[1] Be wary of falling into the mindset of, "Oh, can't I just cancel that meeting? I have nothing to say today." This is likely a trap as you may miss an opportunity to listen to the other person who may actually have something to say. It might be that last piece in the puzzle (or in your blind spot) that you have not thought about—and that helps you and them to come up with a new idea.

By acknowledging their views and needs, and by identifying shared interests, we are building trust. It changes the dynamic of any negotiation.

The mutual respect and confidence that comes from trust puts all parties on a level playing field, where no one has more power than another. This is just what we need to make up for the 6th P. Like in a tango, the lead "dancer" often changes, drawing on the expertise of each "P" at relevant moments. The baton is passed from "P" to "P" as they co-create *options* that provide solutions satisfying the *interests* of all people at the healthcare table.[1]

In contrast, a siloed approach is driving over- and under-care, ineffective resource utilization—with resources in the wrong places—and delays in accessing diagnostics and care. Ultimately, this is driving up costs and limiting the patients' (consumers') timely access to effective products.[105] What we want is the right medicines for the right people at the right time.

During our time together in the pharmaceutical industry, Verena and I developed such an MPC program for medical teams at global, regional and local levels. It was our first joint project, growing our joint *purpose* to fight cancer with larger teams. After involving more than 200 colleagues, across three continents, it has changed how teams interact with the 5P health care community at large. In practice, it has helped them break down the walls of "only" presenting scientific data transactionally, and move toward a collaborative model of engagement with physician-scientists as individuals. The upcoming last breakout box highlights how this can work in practice.

Transcend a barrier and co-create new options toward patient benefit.

The result was that the medical teams were often welcomed with an open door when they visited a physician, for example, as they were confident that the engagement would go beyond the evidence and deliver something for them that they didn't have previously. In short, it created value.

To exemplify how walls between 5P actors can show up in people's day job realities, let's share a real-life happening between an academic thought leader professor and a medical director at a pharmaceutical company. Let's call them Prof Doo (🏛 academia) and Dr Swift (💊 pharma).

CREATING PURPOSE AND REMOVING
HURDLES FOR PATIENT-CENTRIC SOLUTIONS

🏛 **Prof Doo:**	Hi Dr Swift, great to see you.
💊 **Dr Swift:**	Likewise, Prof Doo; it's been a while.
🏛 **Prof Doo:**	We wanted to follow up and plan for a meeting at our hospital so that we can brainstorm ideas around how to study some of your new pipeline compounds for our patients suffering from the cancer of the big toe, who today, really have no options left once they fail standard of care.
💊 **Dr Swift:**	Well, I'm so sorry to say, but I discussed it internally after our last meeting and unfortunately, I can't really entertain and meet you around this because cancer of the big toe is not in the company's strategy. So, if at all, this needs to be an IST (investigator-sponsored trial). Also, compliance is very strict and told me I must stay completely hands-off here. Please submit your proposal through our web portal.
🏛 **Prof Doo:**	Hang on, Dr Swift. Are you serious? I don't even know what's in your pipeline. I have so many questions around the new mechanisms of action and how these could fit into our latest digital tech coming out of our institution's lab.
💊 **Dr Swift:**	I could send you some recent posters and the slides from our investor call that describe some of it.
🏛 **Prof Doo:**	That's not what I mean. I am talking about meeting to brainstorm and discuss what is best for our patients. I don't have the answers yet; it's a matter of putting together your knowledge on new compounds and our experience with this disease. I am talking about talking to each other and thinking together. That is not a matter of compliance.
💊 **Dr Swift:**	I am so sorry.
🏛 **Prof Doo:**	Ok, let's recap why we scheduled this call in the first place. Can we agree on the following? We have the patients, we have the scientific disease knowledge, and we have a new digital tech coming along. You have the knowledge and expertise on novel mechanisms of actions and drugs that could be explored for this disease. So far so good?
💊 **Dr Swift:**	So, what if we call it a "disease exchange meeting" to learn about latest data from each other?
🏛 **Prof Doo:**	I like this idea and new turn in our conversation. Let's put first things first: what's the problem in the current patient pathway that we need to solve and what are our options to tackle them? Maybe this leads to a study idea, and once we discuss a potential study design, we can discuss who the best owner and legal sponsor for the study should be.
💊 **Dr Swift:**	Happy to hear we are charting a path forward here and are keeping it on medical, scientific terms first. How about meeting next month?

The conclusion of this case? It's usually not a compliance story. It's rarely a money conversation either. It is always around finding a common *purpose* and co-creating *options* on how to make a win-win solution work for real patients. That's what we call a song sheet for collaborative value creation to make patient centricity a reality. For all.

Lastly, great novel solutions only really work when there is a *commitment* to implement. Clear actions and accountability from all parties are required. To minimize the likelihood that one or more parties doesn't follow through on their commitment, it is imperative not to focus too quickly on the first, seemingly best, idea on the table. Pause and create time and space to reflect. There's a real risk of missing others' perspectives and failing to discover an even better option, if only the conversation had continued for longer. Sometimes, this means pausing and regrouping at a later date, such as in the example of Verena's Korean payer negotiation in Chapter 4. However, let's not fool ourselves. There are times where the common ground is too thin and a joint solution too far on the horizon. And that's okay.

Despite all your best efforts, there are occasions when you will be unable to reach an agreement and you decide to take a separate route from the people you were just engaging with. Considering wisely your *alternatives* outside of this deal on the table may indeed be your best solution. Among the several routes you could take, or other companies, partners, and hospitals to work with, choosing the best "alternative" is what the negotiation community refers to as your BATNA: *the best alternative to a negotiated agreement.*

DANCING THROUGH THE FINISH LINE

While the 6th P is still missing, the success of this MPC song sheet continues resonating over and over again since we started applying it to the health care tango about a decade ago. It catalyzes positive energy and brings light into the darkest moments when we think, "Is change in health care really possible?" The answer is squarely and honestly: "Yes!"

Let's share a secret here: we, and you as health care leaders, have a tremendous starting advantage. Our common *purpose* is crystal clear: improving and caring for patients' lives. Agreed? As you're holding and reading this book, we're confident you can subscribe to this.

Well, then you may only be one *curiosity question* away from opening up a new partnership that drives you toward a collaborative tango.

Figure 6.4: Celebrating successes is so important—maybe with a tango?

"REMEMBER, WINNING ISN'T THE ONLY THING. YOU ALSO NEED TO DEVELOP A GREAT VICTORY DANCE."

Changing our healthcare infrastructure and systems approach takes time, for which we have a shared responsibility. As a start, we can all take the time to continue pulling back that curtain, getting to know our fellow 5Ps as individuals by becoming more curious and building relationships for the long term as we will need to work together over time to foster change.

Will *you* take your first step today?

The story of how we (Suzanne and Verena) met, and why we are writing this book chapter together, is a wonderful testament to the magic of the seven steps. The more we shared our *interests* about this *Next Tango*, and did so with *curiosity* and open *communication* around all the possible *options* for this joint project—always with strong benchmarking *legitimacy* on why this patient guide is so terribly needed, and anchoring it in our strong joint *purpose* of always putting patients first—the better our deal and the stronger our book would be at the end. It was done with a strong *commitment* to follow through, and without ever a need to go down *alternate* roads.

In other words, the seven-step framework transcended our *relationship* from being short-sighted and transactional to one based on collaboration and continued value enhancing.

As we wrap up this final chapter, here are some questions to consider in relation to the 6th P we will never find.

- **Step up:** Are you making yourself heard and allowing others to feel heard? This means asking a question, actively listening, and acknowledging the response. Remember that acknowledgment doesn't mean agreement, but it's critical that the other parties also feel heard.

- **Trust:** What is your contribution to trust building in a relationship? Is your focus on value creation for better patient solutions? Do you help to remove hurdles?

- **Win-win:** What have you started and stopped doing lately? Are you clear about your purpose and interests? Are you exploring enough options together to grow the joint ground of value for all? Remember, a zero-sum game where everyone insists on their position destroys value.

- **The 1% rule:** What is the *one* thing you can do differently that can make a big impact for you and the other parties?

- **Things. Take. Time.:** Do you allow yourself to ask for support? Coaching? Pulling in someone from whom you can learn? As a leader, do you help others around you? Sometimes, that means pushing back on your boss who wants quick results, or, as a patient, pushing back on your doctor because you still have lots of questions unanswered.

The last step toward patient centricity—*quo vadis?*

By Hanna Boëthius and Verena Voelter

*"Never doubt that a small group of thought-
ful, committed people can change the world.
Indeed, it is the only thing that ever has."*

~ MARGARET MEAD

Coming off dancing this *Next Tango* of patient centricity, we are propelling ourselves into the future. The key question is: What is our healthcare world likely to look like a decade from now?

How can we inject more care into healthcare? How can we rein in skyrocketing costs? And how can we minimize the frustration that continues to spread like wildfire? Significant barriers still obstruct our path: entrenched silos, misaligned incentives, and a lack of shared understanding that hinders the progress toward patient-centered care. Even within each stakeholder group, we face resistance. Whether it's a doctor's view that system change, not coaching, is what's needed, or a patient's struggle to navigate complex health information alone. Payers, policymakers, and pharma face strong headwinds linked to affordability, livelihoods, and regulations, bringing along hostile behaviors more often than not.

We arrive at a pivotal realization: to fix our plaguing healthcare systems, we must truly place patients at the center of health care by embracing collaboration as our guiding principle!

Today, our healthcare system is a tapestry woven from the contributions of diverse stakeholders—the 5Ps: patients, providers, pharma, payers, and policymakers. Tomorrow, as we look toward a patient-centered future, we see that no single actor can solve the challenges of health care alone. Patient centricity is a synchronized dance, a collaboration where every step counts.

Throughout this practical guide, we have looked deeper into the intricacies of this health care "tango." We explored how patients, empowered to be active participants, are the very heartbeat of the system. We saw how providers, embracing their roles as compassionate listeners and innovative practitioners, can foster more meaningful connections with patients. Pharma, with its responsibility to develop treatments that improve lives, can adopt patient-centered approaches that prioritize patient voices throughout the research and development process. Payers hold the key to shifting from fee-for-service models to value-based care, rewarding outcomes that truly matter to patients. And policymakers, crafting the framework of healthcare, have the power to create a more inclusive and patient-centric environment by encouraging collaboration and data sharing.

*As we navigated these pages together,
we hope you join us to realize that there
is earnest cause for optimism.*

We have identified a song sheet to orchestrate this complex tapestry toward more aligned interests and incentives: the seven steps of multi-party collaboration, anchored in a common purpose and fueled by curiosity. From inspiring examples of patient-led research to outcome-based contracting, we see the 5Ps finding new ways to dance together, forming the backbone of a more patient-centered future.

Henry Ford said, *"Coming together is a beginning. Keeping together is progress. Working together is success."* The way we all can make this *Next Tango* a success is by adopting a radically new mindset. Ask yourself: What can I contribute to make patient centricity a reality? How can I dismantle barriers to collaboration, break down walls of mistrust, and create space for open dialogue? How can I maintain focus on shared goals, aligning incentives, and foster curiosity and commitment? By doing so, all stakeholders along the 5P value chain can create a healthcare system that delivers on its promise: better health for patients, better outcomes for all.

Here, we invite you to step into this collaborative journey. Think of yourself as a part of this intricate health care tango, where each move matters. What steps will you take to embrace collaboration and make patient centricity not just a concept but a reality? Together, we can transform healthcare into a system that truly serves the patient above all else.

Reflecting on this fantastic journey of co-authoring *The Next Tango* with a small group of dedicated health care leaders, we have come to believe that health care in ten years will be smarter, more collaborative, and fully patient-centered.

It is the only way forward. We don't have any other alternative. And we have no time to lose.

Are you in?

ACKNOWLEDGMENTS
and AUTHOR BIOS

Hanna Boëthius, MSc and Verena Voelter, MD would like to sincerely thank all the great supporters and sounding boards that helped forge a book on self-care and patient centricity, based on the idea of buying a handbag on Zurich's *Bahnhofstrasse*! There are too many to name them all. However, a few spent hours of their precious time reading early drafts of this *Next Tango*. Ezgi Yilmaz has supported us with graphics and updates on healthcare spending and waste analytics. And a mature manuscript is only as good as a solid beta reading review; we are thankful to Magda Witschi for offering us her sharp mind in this regard. Transforming a manuscript into a book is the magic of Scott MacMillan's team at Grammar Factory. A true entrepreneur-to-author at heart, Scott is our perfect tango partner in terms of bringing the health care dance to people's bookshelves. Thank you for your agility, professional support, and resilience in catering to our multicultural and multilingual backgrounds, and our multiple sets of readers! Lastly, this *Next Tango* wouldn't exist without the incredible partnership of our fellow authors. We are forever grateful to them for having trusted us on this book adventure and for their undisputed leadership in the patient-centric VBHC transformation. We need more like you out there!

Hanna and Verena can be reached at **5PHealthCareSolutions. com** for consulting, coaching, and moderating support. They also welcome direct messages via comments on their LinkedIn profiles:

- Hanna: https://www.linkedin.com/in/hannaboethius/
- Verena: https://www.linkedin.com/in/verena-voelter-md-44aa4116/

CLAUDIA CANELLA, MA AND CLAUDIA WITT, MD, MBA

Professor Claudia Witt is a medical doctor and epidemiologist with a passion for digital health and participatory research projects. She is director of the Digital Society initiative at the University of Zurich (UZH) and serves as director of the Institute for Complementary and Integrative Medicine at the University Hospital of Zurich (USZ).

Claudia Canella is a qualitative health researcher specializing in participatory research at the UZH / USZ Institute of Complementary and Integrative Medicine.

They state:

"We both believe that meaningful value creation for all stakeholders can only be achieved through collaborative partnerships in research and health care.

We thank all the stakeholders who participated in the DITRAS, PEMS, and RIMA projects for their collaboration and valuable contribution. We acknowledge the other research team members in those projects: Jürgen Barth, Anita Thomae, Anna Tietjen, Jesús Lopez-Alcalde, Yan Yuqian, and Carina Braun. Share your thoughts with us at claudia.canella@usz.ch.

- Claudia Canella: https://www.linkedin.com/in/claudia-canella-556b2596/
- Claudia Witt: https://www.linkedin.com/in/claudia-m-witt-aa1a72185/

NIENKE FEENSTRA, MPHARM

Nienke Feenstra is a long-term pharmaceutical leader with a broad geographic reach while keeping her compass on Value-Based Health Care transformation.

In her view, when leading country teams in Hungary, Poland, and France, the aim is to build the most patient-focused and sustainable pharmaceutical business, in which innovation at large can be incorporated and recognized. That starts by defining ambitious goals in terms of value, and orienting all strategies, tactics, and processes toward that, fueled by the power of purpose, and delivered by cross-functional teams.

She states:

"I am passionate about delivering sustainable results through partnerships with all stakeholders in health care. The starting point of delivering results is adding true value for patients, regardless of the role I have been in and whether it was a local, national or global role.

Throughout the course of my studies and working life, I have been inspired by so many across the full spectrum of 5Ps who have shared and stimulated the impact we have had on patients' lives, and I would like to thank you all—you know who you are. I have contributed to this book to share these lessons and hopefully amplify them."

- Nienke: https://www.linkedin.com/in/nienkefeenstra2/

CAITLIN MASTERS, MPH

Caitlin Masters is a value-based care expert and consultant, grounded in real-world experience. In her opinion, health is everything!

She states:

"Creating a sustainable health care delivery system for future generations is what ignites my passion for Value-Based Health Care and is the driving force on why I believe this book, written in simple terms, will help us move the needle forward.

The early believers of driving high-quality healthcare through collaboration created the foundation of VBHC. It is through you and through serendipitous relationships that brought me to my passion. Thank you to those early believers and to my many mentors for the inspiration, confidence, and belief that a better, more sustainable healthcare system is possible.

Most importantly, for my daughter, Fiona, may you benefit from your mama's passion. Remember, if you want to go fast, go alone. If you want to go far, go together."

- Caitlin: https://www.linkedin.com/in/caitlin-masters/

PAUL SHERRINGTON, PHD

Dr Sherrington has dedicated his working life to the field of hematological malignancies. He initially focused on the cytogenetics and the molecular genetics of leukemia at the University of Cambridge, the MRC Laboratory of Molecular Biology, and then the Haematology Department at the Royal Liverpool University Hospital.

He states:

"For the next fourteen years, I worked in the biopharmaceutical sector, most recently at Celgene (recruited by Verena!) where I was able to translate my provider experience into several roles in medical affairs teams, broadening my clinical research scope of lymphomas, myeloma, and myeloid diseases. Since 2021, I have been involved with the DIDACT Foundation and recently was appointed CEO of Accelerating Clinical Trials Limited.

Making a positive difference for people with devastating diseases is what motivates me every day. I thank Verena and Hanna for giving me this opportunity to contribute to this novel book, and for their critical eye and contribution to the manuscript."

- Paul: https://www.linkedin.com/in/paul-sherrington-b6599822/

SUZANNE ROBINSON, PHD

Dr Robinson's career in health care began in scientific research before transitioning to medical affairs in the biopharmaceutical industry and laterally building a strategic medical consultancy team within the communications sector. As an alumna of the Harvard Negotiation Program, Suzanne partnered with Verena to lead large-scale negotiation skills training programs globally.

She states:

"My mom used to say, 'If you don't ask, then you don't get.' Next time you are in a seemingly blocked negotiation, be curious, ask a question. Propelled by patient centricity, I started my journey into health care as a daughter and wrote this book as a mother. Collaboration starts at home and thank you to my son, Isaac, for everything you teach me daily, and for your patience and kindness, enabling me to be a part of *The Next Tango*.

I am privileged to have played a part in the development of this book. Thank you to old and new connections for providing support along this journey."

- Suzanne: https://www.linkedin.com/in/suzanne-robinson-b853279/

GLOSSARY

ACO: Accountable Care Organizations

ACS: Acute Coronary Syndrome

ADA: International, American Diabetes Association

AI: Artificial Intelligence

ALS: Amyotrophic Lateral Sclerosis

API: Application Programming Interfaces

AMI: Acute Myocardial Infarction

ART: Antiretroviral Therapy

BATNA: Best Alternative to a Negotiated Agreement

BPCI-A: Bundled Payments Care Improvement—Advanced Program

CBER: Center for Biologics Evaluation and Research

CDER: Center for Drug Evaluation and Research Real-World
Evidence

CMS: Center of Medicare and Medicaid Services

CNIL: Commission Nationale de l'Informatique et des Libertés

CROMS: Clinician-Reported Outcome Measures

DAA: Direct-Acting Antivirals

DITRAS: Digital Training to Support Cancer Patients to Apply
Self-Care

DOC: Diabetes Online Community

EFPIA: European Federation of Pharmaceutical Industries and
Associations

EMA: European Medicines Agency

ePRO: Electronic Patient-Reported Outcome

ER: Emergency Room

EU: European Union

FDA: Food and Drug Administration

FFS: Fee-For-Service

GMP: Good Manufacturing Practice

GP: General Practitioner

HbA1c: Hemoglobin A1C (showing average blood glucose levels over the past 3 months)

HCP: Health Care Provider

HEOR: Health Economics Outcomes Research

HHS: Department of Health & Human Services in the US

H@H: Hospital at Home

HHH: Hospital to Home Hurdle

HTA: Health Technology Assessment

H2O: Health Outcomes Observatory

IBD: Inflammatory Bowel Disease

ICD-10: International Statistical Classification of Diseases—10th edition

ICF: Informed Consent Form

ICH: International Council for Harmonisation

IHI: Innovative Health Initiative

IST: Investigator Sponsored Trial

MAA: Marketing Authorization Approval

MBM: Mind Body Medicine

ML: Machine Learning

MPC: Multi-Party Collaboration

MS: Multiple Sclerosis

NORD: National Organization for Rare Disorders

NQMC: National Quality Measures Clearinghouse

OECD: Organisation for Economic Co-operation and Development

OSH: Oak Street Health

PEMS: Participatory Evidence Synthesis in Multiple Sclerosis

PCOR: Patient-Centered Outcome Research

PON: Program on Negotiation

PPP: Public-Private Partnership

PPI(E): Patient and Public Involvement or Patient and Public Involvement and Engagement

PREM: Patient-Reported Experience Measure

PRO: Patient-Reported Outcome (Research)

PROM: Patient-Reported Outcome Measure

QI: Quality Indicator

QoL: Quality of Life

R&D: Research and Development

RIMA: Resource-Oriented Integrative Methods for people with ALS

RPM: Remote Patient Monitoring

ROI: Return on Investment

RVU: Relative Value Unit

RWD: Real-World Data

RWE: Real-World Evidence

SDOH: Social Determinants of Health

SNDS: Smart Network Data Services

SOP: Standard Operating Procedure

TCM: Traditional Chinese Medicine

T1D: Type 1 Diabetes

T2D: Type 2 Diabetes

TD-ABC: Time-Driven Activity-Based Costing

VBHC: Value-Based Health Care

VBC: Value-Based Care

W.A.I.T.: Waiting to Access Innovative Therapies (Indicator)

WEF: World Economic Forum

REFERENCES

Preface: Why patient centricity matters

1. Verena Voelter (2021) *It Takes 5 to Tango: From Competition to Cooperation in Health Care*. Grammar Factory Publishing, an imprint of MacMillan Company Limited

2. Alan Condon (2024) Steward, Cano and more: 5 recent healthcare bankruptcies; 10 June; available at: https://www.beckershospitalreview.com

3. www.oecd.org

4. United Kingdom (UK): Life expectancy at birth from 2012 to 2022; available at: www. statista.com

5. U.S. Life Expectancy 1950-2024; available at: www.macrotrends.net

6. Lisa Hefti, Hanna Boëthius, Verena Voelter et al. (2024) "The Tango to Modern Collaboration and Patient-Centric Value Generation in Health Care—a real-world guide from practitioners for practitioners: A field analysis on Value-Based Health Care of 12 leading institutions worldwide." Curr Med Res Opin (2025) 41; 1

7. RISE VBHC summit (2024); available at: www.risehealth.org

8. Giles Bruce (2023) How Dr. Stephen K. Klasko had a "197-year-old academic medical center thinking like a startup"; 23 January; available at: www.beckerhospitalreview.com

9. Stephen K. Klasko. (2023) *Feelin' Alright: How the Message in the Music Can Make Healthcare Healthier*. Ache Management Publishers

Introduction: A song sheet for individual satisfaction and value generation

10. OECD (2017), *Tackling Wasteful Spending on Health*, OECD Publishing, Paris

11. William H. Shrank et al. (2019) Waste in the US Health Care System—Estimated Costs and Potential for Savings. JAMA; 322(15):1501-1509

12. Michael E. Porter and Elizabeth Olmsted Teisberg. (2006) *Redefining Health Care. Creating Value-Based Competition on Results*. Harvard Business Press

13. www.vbhc.eu

14. Vivek Murthy. Addressing Health Worker Burnout: The U.S. Surgeon General's Advisory on Building a Thriving Health Workforce [Internet] Office of the Surgeon General (OSG) Washington (DC): US Department of Health and Human Services; 2022. Publications and Reports of the Surgeon General

15. Current Priorities of the U.S. Surgeon General; available at: https://www.youtube.com/watch?v=Ak2RNYZwiP4

16. Sharee Johnson (2021) *The Thriving Doctor*. Hambone Publishing

17. Vinayak K. Prasad and Adam S. Cifu (2019) *Ending the Medical Reversal. Improving Outcomes, Saving Lives*. A Johns Hopkins Press Health Book

18. Paul DeChant (2024) *How to Improve Health Practice Workplace Conditions*; available at: www.pauldechantmd.com

19. Andrea Austin (2024) *Revitalized: A Guidebook to Following Your Healing Heartline*. The American Campus

20. WEF report on future of jobs report (2023); available at: www.weforum.org

CHAPTER 1: The Patient view

21. The British Medical Journal; available at: www.bmj.com

22. Diabetologica; available at: www.diabetologia-journal.org

23. Sue Robins (2022) *Ducks in a Row—Health Care Reimagined*. Bird Communications Canada

24. An event report from an official G20 side event; available at: https://ncdalliance.org/sites/default/files/resource_files/T20_Report_2023.09.07.pdf

25. Anne Cooper et al (2018) Language matters. Addressing the use of language in the care of people with diabetes: position statement of the English Advisory Group. Diabetic Medicine. 35(12):1630-4

26. Eric Topol (2019) *Deep Medicine*. Basic Books, New York

27. JW Shao et al (2024) Development and Application of an AI-based Empathic Language Teaching and Evaluation System for Doctor-patient Communication. Chinese General Practice. Dec 5;27(34):4315

28. The 5PEP program; available at: https://5phealthcaresolutions.com/index.php/5pep/

29. Stephen S. Coughlin et al. (2020) Health Literacy, Social Determinants of Health, and Disease Prevention and Control

30. Laura Schang et al (2021) What makes a good quality indicator set? A systematic review of criteria. Int J Qual Health Care 33(3):mzab107

31. Ana Renka Darby et al (2024) Physicians' perspectives on clinical indicators: systematic review and thematic synthesis. Int J Qual Health Care 36(3):mzae082

32. How do PREMs and PROMs work together? Available at: www.cemplicity.com

33. Loren Eiseley (1979) The Star Thrower. Houghton Mifflin Harcourt; adaptation from https://en.wikipedia.org/wiki/The_Star_Thrower

CHAPTER 2: The Provider view

34. Fenke Hoekstra et al (2020) Panel SCIGPC. A review of reviews on principles, strategies, outcomes and impacts of research partnerships approaches: a first step in synthesising the research partnership literature. Health Research Policy and Systems;18(1):51

35. Patient-Centered Outcomes Research Institute. PCORI. (2019) Annual report. Patient-Centered Outcomes Research Institute

36. ECSA (2015) Ten Principles of Citizen Science, Berlin

37. Claudia Canella (2024) Participatory research in integrative cancer medicine: Exploiting the potentials and addressing the challenges. [Dissertation] in press

38. Sara Colomer-Lahiguera et al. (2023) Patient and public involvement in cancer research: A scoping review. Cancer Med Jul;12(14)

39. James D. Harrison et al (2019) Patient stakeholder engagement in research: A narrative review to describe foundational principles and best practice activities. Health Expectations 22(3):307-16

40. Marissa Bird et al (2020) Preparing for patient partnership: A scoping review of patient partner engagement and evaluation in research. Health Expectations 23(3):523-39

41. Carolina Bergerum et al (2019) How might patient involvement in healthcare quality improvement efforts work—A realist literature review. Health Expectations 22(5):952-64

42. Trisha Greenhalgh et al (2019) Frameworks for supporting patient and public involvement in research: Systematic review and co-design pilot. Health Expectations 22(4):785-801

43. Janet E. Jull JE et al (2019) A review and synthesis of frameworks for engagement in health research to identify concepts of knowledge user engagement. BMC Medical Research Methodology 19(1):211

44. Marie-Michèle Pratte et al (2023) Researchers' experiences with patient engagement in health research: a scoping review and thematic synthesis. Research Involvement and Engagement 9(1):22

45. Ashokan Arumugam et al (2023) Patient and public involvement in research: a review of practical resources for young investigators. BMC Rheumatology 7(1):2

46. Jennifer L. Shirk et al. (2012) Public Participation in Scientific Research: A Framework for Deliberate Design. Ecology and Society; 17(2)

47. Victoria Maizes et al. (2009) Integrative Medicine and Patient-Centered Care. Explore (NY) 5(5):277-89

48. Robert B. Saper (2017) Integrative Medicine and Health. Med Clin of North Am 101(5):xvii-xviii

49. The DITRAS project. Digital Training to support cancer patients to apply selfcare methods; available at: https://www.usz. ch/fachbereich/komplementaere-und-integrative-medizin/ forschung/online-schulung-akupressur/

50. The PEMS project. Participatory evidence synthesis in multiple sclerosis and complementary therapies. (2024) Institute for Complementary and Integrative Medicine, University Hospital of Zurich; available at: https://osf.io/ys7xt/

51. The Cochrane Collaboration, available at: www.cochrane.org/

52. The RIMA project. Claudia Canella et al (2024) Developing a digital mind body medicine supportive care intervention for people with amyotrophic lateral sclerosis using stakeholder engagement and design thinking. Digit Health (10)1–11; eCollection 2024 Jan-Dec

53. Schweizerische Multiple Sklerose Gesellschaft; available at: www.multipleskelorse.ch

54. International Committee of Medical Journal Editors (ICMJE); available at: www.icmje.org

CHAPTER 3: The Pharma view

55. The Antiretroviral Therapy Cohort Collaboration (2017) Survival of HIV-positive patients starting antiretroviral therapy between 1996 and 2013: a collaborative analysis of cohort studies. Lancet HIV 4: e349-356

56. Joana Ferreira et al (2024) Effects of HCV Clearance with Direct-Acting Antivirals (DAAs) on Liver Stiffness, Liver Fibrosis Stage and Metabolic/Cellular Parameters. Viruses 16:371

57. Olivier J. van Not et al (2024) Long term survival in patients with advanced melanoma. JAMA Network Open (2024);7(8): e2426641

58. Duxin Sun et al. (2022) Why 90% of clinical drug development fails and how to improve it? Acta Pharmaceutica Sinica 12(7):3049-3062

59. Patient perspectives can shape trial design; available at: www.iqvia.com

60. Estelle Jobson et al (2024) Embedding patient engagement in the R&D process of a life sciences company through co-creation with a patient expert R&D board: a case study. Research Involvement and Engagement 10:116

61. Personal communication from the author

62. Darren A. DeWalt et al (2004) Literacy and health outcomes: a systematic review of the literature. J Gen Intern Med Dec;19(12):1228-39

63. How to harness the power of health data to improve patient outcomes (2024) The World Economic Forum, Jan 5

64. Le consortium et sa plateforme AGORiA SANTĒ; available at: www.agoriasante.com

65. Kaiku Health; available at: www.elekta.com

66. Sanna Livanainen S (2023) ePRO symptom follow-up of colorectal cancer patients receiving oxaliplatin-based adjuvant

chemotherapy is feasible and enhances the quality of patient care: a prospective multicenter study. Cancer Res Clin Oncol 149:6875-6882

67. AI-driven diagnosis of rare (hidden) diseases; available at: www.saventic.com

68. The World Economic Forum (2023) The Moment of Truth for Healthcare Spending: How Payment Models can Transform Healthcare Systems. Insight Report, January

69. The World Economic Forum, The Global Coalition in Healthcare; available at: https://initiatives.weforum.org/global-coalition-for-value-in-healthcare/home

70. Hanna Boëthius and Yasmin Dias-Guichot (2023) A conversation on VBHC principles: Value = Outcomes / Cost. 5PFlagship2023 event; available at: https://5phealthcaresolutions.com/index.php/videos/

71. The Health Outcomes Observatory; available at: https://health-outcomes-observatory.eu/

72. PROMs standard sets at ICHOM; available at: https://www.ichom.org/patient-centered-outcome-measures/

CHAPTER 4: The Payer view

73. Caitlin Masters and Verena Voelter (2024) Value-Based Health Care—a 5-sided coin? available at: www.medium.com

74. Marco Bertini and Oded Koenigsberg (2020) *The Ends Game. How smart companies stop selling products and start delivering value*. The MIT Press.

75. Trends in health care spending (2022) available at: www.ama-assn.org

76. CHE Federal Statistical Office—Costs, Financing (2022) available at: https://www.bfs.admin.ch/bfs/en/home/statistiken/gesundheit/kosten-finanzierung.html

77. Eurostat, Health care expenditure by financing scheme (2022) available at: https://ec.europa.eu/eurostat/

78. Pharmaceutical spending, OECD (2022) Available at: https://www.oecd.org/

79. Eurostat, Healthcare expenditure statistics (2020) available at: https://ec.europa.eu/eurostat/

80. William H. Shrank et al (2019) Waste in the US Health Care System: Estimated Costs and Potential for Savings. JAMA Oct 15;322(15):1501-1509

81. Micha Aebi (2024). «30 Prozent der Gesundheitskosten sind reine Verschwendung» 02 June; available at: www.tagesanzeiger.ch

82. Kaspar Schwarzenbach (2024) Schon eine Milliarde mehr: Die Gesundheitskosten steigen weiter steil an. 30 July; available at: www.20min.ch/story/

83. Becker's Hospital Review (2024) Healthcare Finance Trends for 2024: An Updated Look. 26 August; available at: www.beckershospitalreview.com/

84. Stefan Larsson, Jennifer Clawson and Josh Kellar (2023) *The Patient Priority*. McGraw Hill

85. Michael E. Porter and Robert S. Kaplan (2016) How to Pay for Health Care. Bundled payments will finally unleash the competition that patients want. Harvard Business Review Jul-Aug

86. Agency for Healthcare, Research and Quality (AHRQ) About NGC and NQMC; available at: https://www.ahrq.gov/gam/about/index.html

87. Michael E. Porter, Stefan Larsson and Thomas H. Lee (2016) Standardizing Patient Outcomes Measurement. N Engl J Med 2016;374:504-506

88. Jens Deerberg-Wittram and Laura Lüdtke (2016) Diabeter: Value-Based Healthcare Delivery in Diabetes; white paper available at: https://www.studocu.com/en-us/document/carleton-college/health-care-economics/value-based-healthcare-diabeter-white-paper/71568900

89. Pierre Sabouret et al. (2022) Post-discharge and long-term follow-up after an acute coronary syndrome: International Collaborative Group of CNCF position paper. Arch Med Sci Jun 23;18(4):839-854.

90. Didier Romain and Gilard Martine on behalf of ESC (2024) Follow-up management after an acute coronary syndrome. European Society of Cardiology > Councils > Council for Cardiology Practice > CardioPractice

91. Deutscher Herzbericht (2022) available at: www.dgthd.de

92. Niki Katsiki et al (2020) Statin therapy in athletes and patients performing regular intense exercise—Position paper from the International Lipid Expert Panel (ILEP). Pharmacol Res May:155:104719. Epub 2020 Feb 19

93. Mads Börjesson et al. (2006) ESC Study Group of Sports Cardiology: recommendations for participation in leisure-time physical activity and competitive sports for patients with ischaemic heart disease. Cardiovasc Prev Rehabil 13(2):137-49

94. Ana Paula Beck da Silva Etges et al. (2019) An 8-step framework for implementing time-driven activity-based costing in healthcare studies. Eur J Health Econ, Nov;20(8):1133-1145

95. www.tdabcconsortium.com/

96. Centers for Medicare and Medicaid Services BPCI Advanced Evaluation Findings at a Glance (2024) available at: www.cms.gov

97. Die Martiniklinik; available at: www.martini-klinik.de/

98. Burkhardt Beyer (2021) Nichts ist schlimmer als Unklarheit

über das eigene Handeln: PROMS an der Martiniklinik. Vortrag.

99. Meletios Dimopoulos et al. (2009) Long-term follow-up on overall survival from the MM-009 and MM-010 phase III trials of lenalidomide plus dexamethasone in patients with relapsed or refractory multiple myeloma. Leukemia Nov;23(11):2147-52.

100. Remarks by President Obama, President Park Geun-Hye of the Republic of Korea, and Prime Minister Shinzo Abe of Japan After Trilateral Meeting covering the Cancer Moonshot initiative, available at: https://obamawhitehouse.archives.gov/the-press-office/2016/03/31/remarks-president-obama-president-park-geun-hye-republic-korea-and-prime

101. Seung-Lai Yoo et al (2018) Improving Patient Access to New Drugs in South Korea: Evaluation of the National Drug Formulary System

CHAPTER 5: The Policymaker view

102. Ezekiel J. Emanuel (2020) Which Country Has the World's Best Health Care? Public Affairs New York

103. Kenneth T. Segel (2017) Bureaucracy Is Keeping Health Care from Getting Better. Harvard Business Review 13 OCT

104. Navigating Healthcare's Bureaucracy System: Clearing the Path for Better Patient Care (2017); available at: https://www.europeancancer.org

105. EFPIA W.A.I.T. indicator; available at: https://efpia.eu/media/vtapbere/efpia-patient-wait-indicator-2024.pdf

106. Paul Wankah et al (2023) Equity Promoting Integrated Care: Definition and Future Development. Int J Integr Care. Oct 19;23(4):6

107. Celia Piquer-Martinez et al (2024) Theories, models and frameworks for health systems integration. A scoping review, Health Policy, Volume 141

108. Patient and public involvement in cancer research: A scoping review

109. Sara Colomer-Lahiguera et al (2023) Jul;12(14):15530-15543

110. 1st International Workshop on Patient and Public Involvement in Cancer Research; available at: https://www.sakk.ch/en/event/workshop-patient-and-public-involvement#tab-program

111. Swiss Clinical Trial Organisation PPI Fact Sheet (2021); available at: https://www.snf.ch/api/media/en/o5yqCe4GPIVk2RUG/scto-factsheet-ppi-en.pdf

112. European Medicines Agency (EMA); available at: www.ema.europa.eu

113. Rosanne Janssens et al. (2023) How can patient preferences be used and communicated in the regulatory evaluation of medicinal products? Findings and recommendations from IMI PREFER and call to action. Front Pharmacol. August 16

114. FDA Real-World Evidence (RWE) Framework (2021); available at: https://www.fda.gov/science-research/real-world-evidence/center-biologics-evaluation-and-research-center-drug-evaluation-and-research-real-world-evidence

115. The Affordable Care Act (2010); available at: https://www.healthcare.gov/glossary/affordable-care-act/

116. Andrea Louise Campbell and Lara Shore-Sheppard (2020) The Social, Political, and Economic Effects of the Affordable Care Act: Introduction to the Issue. The Russell Sage Foundation Journal of the Social Sciences; 6(2)1-40

117. 21st Century Cures Act—Information Blocking Rule; available at: https://www.healthit.gov/topic/information-blocking

118. European Health Data Space (EHDS); available at: https://health.ec.europa.eu/ehealth-digital-health-and-care/european-health-data-space_en

119. The EU Artificial Intelligence Act; available at: https://artificialintelligenceact.eu/

120. The EU data governance act; available at: https://digital-strategy.ec.europa.eu/en/policies/data-governance-act

121. NEW 19 NORD: The Orphan Drug Act Turns 40: NORD Celebrates Its Impact on Rare Diseases (2024) Jan 24; available at: https://rarediseases.org/the-orphan-drug-act-turns-40-nord-celebrates-its-impact-on-rare-diseases/

122. NEW 20 ADA: Colorado's Insulin Copay Cap: A Foundation to Build Upon (2019) 9 JUL; available at: www.t1international.com

123. Regulation on Health Technology Assessment; available at: https://health.ec.europa.eu/health-technology-assessment/

124. The Blood Cancer UK Policy Panel; available at: https://bloodcancer.org.uk

125. Leukemia UK call for government cancer strategy; available at: https://www.leukaemiauk.org.uk/election-manifesto-campaign/

126. The ONC's Cures Act Final Rule on Interoperability and Patient Access at HealthIT.gov; available at: https://www.healthit.gov/topic/oncs-cures-act-final-rule

127. The Evidence Base (2024) ICH reflection paper marks milestone in harmonization of real-world evidence use in medicines regulation (2024); available at: https://www.evidencebaseonline.com/

The 6th P

128. Zeev Neuwirth (2023) *Beyond the Walls: Megatrends, Movements and Market Disruptors Transforming American Healthcare.* Advantage Media Group

129. Roger Fisher and William (Bill) Ury (1981). *Getting to Yes: Negotiating agreement without giving in.* Boston, Houghton Mifflin. 2nd edition reference: Roger Fisher, William (Bill) Ury and Bruce Patton (2006). *Getting to Yes* (2nd ed.). Penguin Putnam

130. William (Bill) Ury (1993) *Getting Past No*. Random House LLC
     US
131. Lifetime risk estimates calculated by the Cancer Intelligence
     Team at Cancer Research UK 2023; available at: www.
     cancerresearchuk.org
132. National Cancer Institute, Cancer Trends Progress Report
     (2022); available at: https://progressreport.cancer.gov/end/
     mortality
133. Our World in Data. Death rate from cancer (1950 to 2022);
     available at: https://ourworldindata.org
134. Béatrice Schaad et al (2023) (In)hospitalités hospitalières. RMS
     éditions

*Note. All weblink references have been accessed between August
and October 2024. The authors do not retain any responsibility
for accuracy or persistence of content related to these links.*